I0522154

WHICH PATH TOWARD ETERNITY?

A Search for Truth

GEORGE BUKOW

Nihil Obstat: Reverend Denis N. Nakkeeran, S.T.L.

Imprimatur: <u>Seán P. Cardinal O'Malley, O.F.M., Cap. Archbishop</u> of Boston

Date: April 24, 2023

Which Path Toward Eternity?
A Search for Truth
© 2019, 2023 by George Bukow

ISBN: 979-8-9896056-0-6 (print)
ISBN: 979-8-9896056-1-3 (ebook)

All references to the Bible are from the
New American (Catholic) Bible: St. Joseph Edition

All rights reserved. Without limiting the rights under copyright reserved above, no part of this publication may be reproduced, stored in or introduced into a retrieval system, or transmitted, in any form, or by any means (electronic, mechanical, photocopying, recording, or otherwise) without the prior written permission of both the copyright owner and the above publisher of this book.

ACKNOWLEDGMENTS

This book is the result of years of growing, writing and responding to the desire and inspiration to help others achieve their eternal salvation. I consider no other goal more important or more pleasing to the eternal God Who has made us with an insatiable desire to possess Him and be with Him for all eternity. That I have been given the opportunity to participate in such an endeavor I consider a great blessing and pray that my efforts will not be found wanting.

A special thanks goes to my close friend and mentor, Professor Kemoh Salia-Bao, who first suggested that I coalesce all of my previous writings, along with new material, into a book that could provide information and insight so sorely lacking in today's world. Without his help the path would have been much more difficult.

I thank my wife, Mary, for her constant and loving support of my work and hope that she will be satisfied with the final result.

CONTENTS

AUTHOR'S PREFACE

In order to better introduce my book to potential readers I would like to present the concerns which prompted me to write the book and to indicate my rationale for the way I have structured the content.

One of the most frustrating aspects of living in today's world is the need to separate truth from fiction in what one is told, either directly or through an all-pervasive media which blares out its talking points and sacrosanct assertions. This is especially true in the realm of faith and religion.

Read any book, listen to any would-be purveyor of knowledge and the listener is immediately faced with asking oneself "Is that really true?" The fact that few actually do ask the question is indicative of a serious lack in intellectual training and discernment. There is also an increasingly hostile response to honest inquiry and the perceived impertinence of questioning what has frequently been ordained as society's determination of what is to be believed.

In matters of faith and morals the boundaries have long ago become blurred, as long-standing imperatives and accepted norms have been questioned. Concurrently, relativism has gained greater stature and the eager adherents subscribe to new "truths and insights."

From the perspective of one who has been rigorously schooled in logic and science it appears to me that many are on a wrong path. My training as an electrical engineer for over thirty years and as a professor of physics for over twenty years has given me the capability to ask the hard questions, separate the facts from the suppositions, and always search for the truth. I have examined a number of sources, listed in the bibliography, and have acquired a baseline of knowledge and understanding that allows me to help those who want to determine a pathway toward that truth.

Often have I heard untruths about my Catholic faith, historical inaccuracies, specious moral assertions not grounded in rigorous scriptural interpretations but emanating from fertile minds wishing a new order more in keeping with their desires. In the minds of many, God has become more believable when put into a form more adaptable to human exhortations. We hear statements like "Why didn't He make us so that we would more easily follow His commands?" Why does He allow so much suffering?" "How could He have allowed that to happen?"

Anther concern is the very limited knowledge many have about their Christian faith, God's relation with His chosen people, the Jewish nation, and the historical records relating to Jesus, the Church He established and the history of Christianity through the ages. Without knowledge, many go through life making poor decisions and becoming disillusioned and unable to effectively combat the incessant demands of a secular world.

In the Foreword of the book I address in some depth the question, "Why are we here?" In the ensuing discussion I look at the options we can propose to answer the question. Following directly is a discussion of God. What attributes does He have? What can we say to those who do not believe that He exists? Has He made Himself known to us in any way?

The history of the Jewish people then becomes central to our discussion. In prophecy we see the announced coming of a Savior for the human race and the coming in time of that Savior, claiming, as no other, to be the Son of God.

The chapters of the book then proceed to enunciate the historical record of Jesus Christ, His life, death and resurrection from the dead, and His ascension into heaven. Then follows the record of the Church He established, the Roman Catholic Church, the history of that church and the results of the Orthodox separation from the Roman Church and the following Protestant Reformation.

The purpose, always, is to accurately present the knowledge needed for people of faith to confidently embrace what they believe and live in accordance with the teachings of that faith. The second part of the book looks at what God has asked of those who would follow the way enunciated by Christ for out salvation.

Before the coming of Jesus, the Scripture states that the people walked in darkness, but then beheld the Light. Many today still walk in darkness. They frequently lack the knowledge or the willingness to seek the Light. God grant that this book may help at least a few to see that Light!

George Bukow

FOREWORD

It can be fruitful at times to think about the meaning of the word eternity. Something that never ends is easy to say but much harder to truly comprehend. From the Book of Sirach in the Bible we read, "The sum of man's days is great if it reaches 100 years; like a drop of water, like a grain of sand are those few years among the days of eternity". *Sir 18:7-8.*

We live in a world of change. We try to hold back the clock, but it continues on oblivious to our efforts. But the clock recording our earthly existence does come to a stop at the moment of our death, when our souls experience the awareness of the Divine. The path which then unfolds before us we can only conjecture, but unfold it will. We cannot say with certainty what path we will be on, but the effort to determine that path will have already been completed. To understand how this will be, we need to address three fundamental questions. How did we get here? Why are we here? Where are we going?

Most people don't spend much time thinking about these questions. They, in many cases, may have come up with perfunctory answers like, "I believe in God"; "God made me like I am. I do the best I can and I think I will be all right"; "I don't believe in God. I think science will eventually be able to explain how the universe started and God will be irrelevant."

People of faith will perhaps say that, "I have accepted Jesus as my Savior and I am assured of salvation". Others will say that, "I believe in a loving God Who would never condemn someone to eternal damnation." Still others will state their belief in a loving God Who has bought them at a great price and has promised them eternal life if they love Him and keep His commandments.

But what is the Truth? Reason tells us that they cannot all be true. They are contradictory. Are we to assume that what we may believe is right and that others who believe differently are wrong? And that others will assume the same thing about what they believe?

Up until the second half of the last century religious belief for most was grounded in Judeo-Christian Tradition and a large segment of our society supported it. Beginning with the "sexual revolution" of the late 60's and 70's traditional norms began to be questioned and long-standing rules of conduct were denigrated and abandoned by many, particularly the young. At the same time there ensued a breakdown of strong family ties, a weakened religious formation and the rise of a virulent atheistic subculture.

With the coming of the 21st Century the situation has gotten much worse. Recent studies have shown that perhaps one-quarter of the population have no religious affiliation. There is continuous agitation by determined activists to preach a "new gospel' rooted not in absolute Truth but evolving from a relativistic society where good is determined from the will of the majority and norms of conduct no longer adhere to hallowed and sacred principles.

Older members of our population have largely not accepted many of the proposed changes because they were raised at a time when traditional beliefs were strongly held and the benefit of those beliefs were clearly seen to have worked toward the benefit and happiness of all. What is greatly lacking in today's young is a clear understanding of their traditions and the importance of how their conduct will affect their happiness both now and in eternity.

Many in today's society will not have good answers to the three questions proposed above.

1) Where did we come from?
2) Why are we here?
3) Where are we going?

They have fashioned their own ideas about God and why they are here. They blithely assume all will be well with them in any future life that may come. Their false teachers have filled them with halcyon visions of a world in which they are right and those teachers of the past are no longer to be accepted.

This book addresses the issue from another perspective. Eventually, all of us will die. As we enter eternity there will be three possible outcomes to our existence in this life.

The first outcome, or path that we may travel, is into oblivion, into nothingness. This is the expectation of those who believe that there is no intelligent Designer (God) and that our universe is one of many universes, one that just happens to be tuned to support life. They propose no adequate explanation for the Big Bang. The second way is to pass into an afterlife of bliss with a loving God Who has prepared that life for us from all eternity. The third way is to pass to an eternal existence without God, without love, without hope.

How then do we determine the Truth? The aim of this book is to show a pathway toward the Truth. Each searcher must then tread their own path toward truth. In seeking truth, the greatest impediment to finding truth is our own egotism and selfishness. We can be blinded by the enticements of the world and choose to not think about eternity. We can avoid searching for truth because we don't want to find something which will require us to change our lifestyle. We can ignore the issue entirely and just take our chances when we die.

I truly believe that many are not searching for Truth. They have accepted what they believe to be true for them. Whether it is actually true is not a question they actively seek to answer. They continue down their path toward that moment when eternity begins.

Why am I writing this book? I believe each of us is here for a purpose and to fulfill that purpose we must use the gifts we have been given to become caring and loving individuals. For some, that may be overcoming severe impediments and obstacles, enduring hardships and striving unceasingly to be the best they can be. For others, it may be using their gifts to help others overcome their trials and misfortunes so as to achieve a better and fuller life.

I have been greatly blessed with a depth of belief, a grace-filled life filled with love and good fortune. I have now reached that time where I am committed to giving of the wisdom and joy which I experience, with the hope that I can help others, who I know are struggling with demons, both physical and spiritual. I do this, not as one who seeks to impart hidden knowledge or new insights that I alone possess but rather, to point, as best I can, to the Truth, the wisdom of the past. I then exhort others to seek sincerely that Truth and follow where it leads them. Many have followed a similar path and I have no doubt that readers of this book can do so also.

How does one find the Truth? One must look with a sincerity of heart, free of biases and preconceived conclusions, using reason and understanding gained from experience and study. I recall when I was enrolled in a university, filled with book knowledge but unable to relate that knowledge in a meaningful way to life. After many scientific endeavors and maturation in the cauldron of life's experience I see much more clearly, albeit still "in a glass darkly", to quote from St. Paul's beautiful passage on love. What I hope to do with that clarity of vision is try to help others avoid mistakes and emptiness, grow in love and appreciation of the gift of life that has been given to them, and embrace the path toward eternity filled with hope.

Walk with me as we search for Truth. Then let that Truth guide you on your way. It is my hope and prayer that those who take the time to read this book and honestly search for the Truth will find what they are looking for—a belief they can abide by and a hope that will sustain them as they pass into eternity.

PART ONE

Introduction

In today's world one is not likely to hear many discussions related to fundamental questions concerning the reasons for our existence and our ultimate destiny. For many, these topics are studiously avoided. For those espousing an atheistic belief, the path embracing a seemingly meaningless purpose for our existence gives no strong reason for serious deliberation. For those embracing a path of belief in God the depth of their belief can vary greatly from very devout to almost casual, with most maintaining a belief that they will be united with God for all eternity. It is probable that few will choose a third path, an eternal existence without God, but that could be an undesired result due to lack of interest or due to an immersion in the world's enticements which suffocates any alternative.

Even under the best circumstances many of our lives are on a never-ending treadmill sprinting from one activity to another, straining to fulfill unending requirements placed upon us and seldom having more than isolated moments to reflect on where we are going and or whether we even know. Even a few decades ago, before the advent of social media, life moved at a much slower pace. Human interactions were much more meaningful. Church and community had a much greater influence on how we lived, what we believed, and on what, ultimately, we hoped to achieve.

Technologically we have advanced greatly. We are awash in information. We can experience things we could never have imagined. For many, life has become a smorgasbord of new thrills and luxuries. And yet, there remain problems. We have not changed human nature. There are still selfishness, greed, injustice, plus a host of new problems stemming from the new technologies. Relationships within families have deteriorated and many of our young adults have lost their moorings and are adrift in a new age of narcissism and hedonism.

We frequently hear references to the "greatest generation", those who shouldered the tremendous sacrifices required to bring us to victory in the Second World War. They came from little in terms of wealth or education but they gave everything because they believed in performing a greater good. No one looks back at their sacrifices and says, "What a shame. They obtained so little from life. Was it worth it?" No one says that because most believe that the many who died have gone to a better place. They were here for a purpose and they achieved that purpose.

But to truly believe what I just wrote we will need to have good answers to three questions: Where did we come from? Why are we here? Where are we going? If we don't have satisfactory answers to these questions how can we make any statement concerning what we hope to achieve in life? How can we be content that we are on the path to eternity that we desire? How can we even know that what we expressed about the greatest generation is true?

To begin to gain answers to the above questions we will need to go back to basics. Did we come from nothing or is there an Intelligent Designer (God) Who created us and placed us here on this earth at this time? If there is a God, why did he create us? If we find an answer how will we know it is true? If God created us for a purpose, what do we need to do to fulfill that purpose? Is life over when we die? What happens after we die?

As we go through the chapters in this book we will lay the groundwork to answer the above questions. We will look at the arguments of those who claim there is no God. We will look at the attributes of God based on philosophy and theology, the nature of Truth, the sources of good and of evil. We will investigate if God has made anything known to us about His Divine Nature.

Central to our culture is the Judeo-Christian tradition and it is that tradition which will be the basis of our exposition. Much of the material is applicable to other cultures, particularly in Part Two. We will trace the emergence of the Jewish people from the paganism and idolatry of the ancient world and the coming of Jesus Christ, claiming as no other, to be the Son of God and the long-promised Messiah of the Jewish people. We will trace the history of the Church He founded and the fractured nature of Christianity as it exists today.

In doing so we will try to correct errors many have come to believe based on faulty information, inadequate instruction, or a serious lack of understanding. A mature grasp of the significance of the above questions is often lacking during childhood and adolescence and the opportunity to engage in such discussions later in life, when the questions can be discussed more completely, can be very rewarding. What will always be required is a sincere attempt on the part of those involved to seek a sound understanding so that necessary changes in conduct and lifestyles can be pursued with enthusiasm and confidence in achieving a positive result.

Even a casual examination of society today reveals a great deal of dissatisfaction, aimlessness, lack of realistic goals and mistake-driven actions taken earlier in life resulting in serious impediments to future happiness. One wonders whether a better preparation for life and a clearer understanding of the consequences of their actions could have resulted in many becoming able to avoid such unfortunate results. The later chapters of this book, in Part Two, discuss areas that require particular attention during the growth of an individual.

We will discuss the presence of evil in the world, suffering, and our responses to it. Many deny the presence of evil spirits and others object that God allows so much suffering in the world. We will try to provide insights from the words of Scripture.

A successful life must be a disciplined life. Control of our emotions is of paramount importance. Without such control our goals can become clouded by our desires for pleasure, riches, or other distractions. We can become fair-weather pilgrims wanting to respond to exhortations stemming from our core beliefs but always pulled astray by passions we have never learned or desired strongly enough to control.

The importance of love in our lives cannot be over emphasized. But it is not a self-centered love. It is a love which focuses on our relations with others, looking to their welfare while at the same time becoming ourselves more caring and considerate individuals. Talk is cheap. Love is demonstrated in actions, not in empty words.

What is the source of happiness? Many seek happiness in material things, in power, in pleasure and end up empty, dissolute and finding out too late that they have failed miserably to develop into the fully alive, loving individuals they were meant to be. What are some of the impediments which will hinder our becoming loving and fulfilled individuals? If we are filled with pride which inflates our accomplishments, if we hold grudges, if we presume that we know best about what is right and wrong for us and give no heed to valid sources contradicting what we are doing, then we become obstacles to our best interests and impervious to changes we need to make in our lives.

For people of faith in God, prayer is paramount. For many, prayer is to be engaged in during times of sorrow or great need. Imagine a young child going to his mother only when he wanted something. Should he not want to thank her for all she has done for him? Should he not look to her for knowledge and counsel and express to her his love? God should not be treated only as a source of things we want. The reality is that we often do not have the wisdom to know what we should ask for. To obtain that wisdom we need to become more godlike and to do that, we need prayer. Prayer provides a pathway to receive grace, allowing us to see more clearly, thus helping us to live our lives in accordance with His will.

The last section of the book deals with our departure from this life into eternity and our preparation for that departure. By that time, we should have determined which of the paths to eternity we expect to follow. We should be fully aware of the reasons for our determination and have put into effect the actions we have determined to pursue. Life can be very uncertain and if we do not take the necessary steps while there is still time we may well end up on a path we did not desire.

In summary, if at the end of our lives as we look back at what we have achieved, what will we want to see? Each of us would be well advised to know early on what we would like to see and to have earnestly tried to make that a reality. We frequently hear stories about those who have squandered their lives chasing ephemeral goals and neglecting family and human relationships. They look back on what could have been and was not. A deacon I once knew frequently visited parishioners in the hospital contemplating imminent death. He heard many regrets. One he did not hear was, "not spending more time at the office".

Chapter One
The Empty Promise of Atheism

Before we can address any of the fundamental questions about our existence, we must address the preeminent question, "Is there a God?" If, as many believe, there is no God and everything we observe and experience is the result of random sequences, with no Intelligent Designer, no meaning, then everything else we might conclude will be largely the result of conjecture and unfounded hypotheses formulated from fertile minds seeking answers that fit their hypotheses.

But where does that leave the average searcher who is not encumbered by a priori biases and who is looking for a basis for their existence. Do they just accept what these oracles of knowledge tell them or do they look for alternatives that may well be much better grounded in observable experience, rigorous exposition and stemming from the intellectual pursuits of the greatest minds the world has ever known?

If you are one of those espousing an atheistic stance wouldn't it be a good idea to look at the issue more thoroughly then you perhaps have done so up until now. Maybe you accepted the atheistic creed because you didn't have a religious background growing up, or because what you learned as part of an established religion just didn't make sense to you. Another look may be fruitful if done with open-mindedness and in a quest for truth.

Perhaps you fall into the category of an agnostic, you just don't know. Perhaps you have been so busy with living your life that thoughts of eternity and God just haven't seemed that important. More importantly, how much thought would you have given to that answer?

The cynic would say, "What's the big deal? You're here today and gone tomorrow. Make the most of it." That answer may not sit too well when one is on their deathbed and finally coming to grips with the question that they have ignored. Where am I going?

We live in a society drowned in information and technological know-how. We pride ourselves in our ability to work hard and prosper from the fruit of our labors. We expect to achieve the best for our children and we probably consider ourselves OK. We may say God, if there is one, will probably be happy with us—we do the best we can and that should be good enough.

If we were to enter into an important contract discussion essential to our well-being no doubt most of us would use the vast array of helpful tools and information we have available to ensure that we are not making a serious mistake, that we have been diligent in our preparation and that we have prepared well in all respects. Why would not that same importance apply to the meaning of our existence, our relationship with God, or conversely, the acceptance of a universe somehow created on its own without God?

There is a choice to be made here, a very important choice. Do I believe that I am here by some random occurrence and that I will pass away at the end of my life like a falling leaf in the autumn? Is the same to be true for my children and all that I have tried to accomplish in my life—random occurrences fading into eternal oblivion? Or is there another choice? Can I believe in a good and loving God who created me and Who will bring me and all who love Him to eternal life?

The Atheism Mirage

Atheism is becoming a more and more strident voice in today's society. It has come a long way from the days of Madeline Murray in the last century and has found a receptive audience in the young, who have been bombarded with an incessant cadence of propaganda extolling the unbridled freedom of unrestricted sex, diminished responsibility and the glorification of self. If we add to that a seriously reduced opportunity for reasoned discussion—in fact, an almost total rejection of such discussions, we have a society adrift in a sea of misinformation and political correctness.

How does one combat a nihilistic philosophy that denies a Creator, a source of all that exists, of all that is true and good? Normally one would look to philosophy, religion and the basic knowledge of right and wrong written on the hearts and minds of everyone. But in an anti-intellectual society with an ever-increasing inability and resistance to any demands on personal time and effort, we are at a decided disadvantage. The result is that many see only a mirage of potential happiness, free of unnecessary restraints, where one is responsible to no one but himself and a discussion of God and first principles is to be consciously avoided.

Perhaps the best way to begin is to look at the results of our current infatuation with atheism. To justify their positions the elite are positing elaborate mathematical models, and an array of arguments attempting to disprove the existence of a God, which by their own postulates they close their minds to at the outset. They propose speculative theories with no credible evidence to support them. They accept the existence of no truths which cannot be explained by science but make little or no effort to investigate miraculous events to determine the truth. The degree of their intellectual bias appears to prevent them from realizing how incongruous it is for them to assume that the God Who created all and keeps it in existence is so knowable as to be understood totally by His creatures.

Well documented miraculous occurrences have occurred frequently over the ages and are dismissed by the skeptics out of hand as being the result of natural phenomena, mass hallucinations or any number of other explanations, none of which are in any way convincing or logical. Nevertheless, they persevere in their disbelief like stoic guardians of their proclaimed truth.

With the general acceptance of the Big Bang Theory—that our universe started approximately 15 billion years ago with a burst of energy, scientists could no longer hold to the existence of an eternal universe and began to postulate mathematical models supporting the possible existence of a large number of universes with one or more "tuned" to be able to support the existence of life on earth as we know it. There is no explanation for what caused the Big Bang and as many new questions are encountered as were there initially. With no way to prove such premises, committed atheists could continue to deny the existence of a Creator and rigidly proclaim that our universe had no Designer and that through eons of time the multiple universes developed to their current states through random sequences and undefined "laws" governing their formation.

Further investigation shows that these so-called random events had numerous fortuitous results, enabling life as we know it today on earth and protecting us from life-ending cataclysms. The ozone layer surrounding the earth, generated by ancient organisms in the ocean, protects us from harmful solar radiation. The earth recycles carbon over long periods of time and the resulting greenhouse gases keep the earth warm enough to sustain life. The earth's magnetic field deflects harmful solar waves. The earth is just the right distance from the sun—a stable, long lasting star, not too small so as to be unstable, but not so massive as to burn too hot and not last long enough to allow the development of planets.

The most astounding event, covered in Gerald Schroeder's book, *The Science of God*, pp 186-189, was the occurrence at the subatomic stage of the initial sequences that led to the formation of mass from that primeval burst of energy—an event which had an infinitesimally small chance to have occurred just by chance. I summarize these facts not to begin a polemical argument with those rigidly maintaining their atheistic views, for that would likely be fruitless, but rather to appeal to those who want to establish some framework within which to live and achieve happiness in their own lives.

Those who make the effort to study the atheist arguments will find that they do not stand up to further scrutiny. Anthony Flew, a well-known atheist, recently changed his position and now believes in God. He has traced his journey from atheism to belief in a Divine Designer of the universe. He has written a book entitled *There is a God*, in which he examines many of the atheistic arguments, a number of which he previously proposed himself, and now finds them unconvincing. Recent scientific findings in the areas of cosmology and biology show that the complexities and interrelationships observed point emphatically to the need of a Designer. The possibility of everything just happening by chance is beyond all rational expectation.

What of those who choose to follow an atheistic life style? Accepting the tenets of their atheistic teachers they may initially be very satisfied in their ability to live as they choose, ignoring any constraints on their actions and smugly assuming that all those who maintain a religious belief are pathetic dupes who lack the intellectual capability to see the folly of their actions. And yet, in quiet moments when the frenetic pace of their lives briefly slows and they ponder what will become of them and their children, they may see that they have nothing to look forward to at the end of life except a self-embraced emptiness that awaits them.

Others, who also profess their atheistic creed, maintain that certain actions, cruelty to children, for example, are wrong. But do they realize that without a God, the source of all goodness and Truth, how can they postulate that anything is right of wrong? Perhaps they would maintain that the random actions of inert particles over eons of time would produce not only the grand universe we see with its laws and complexity but also the bases for right and wrong.

Another point I would like to make is our instinctive response to human kindness and courage in the presence of great danger or hardship. Actions of people who risk great harm to themselves to benefit those in need are a source of great admiration from others. Why? It is because those who do such things do so for a "higher good". It is this higher good that transcends other considerations and prompts them to act as they do. In many cases they refer to their belief in God as a motivating factor, realizing that their current life is a prelude to another life to come. There is a story of a nun who was seen caring for patients with severe physical problems. As a bystander observed her work she said to the nun, "I wouldn't do that for a million dollars." The nun replied, "Neither would I".

Perhaps you are one of those who are living an atheistic life style. The world is your apple and life is good. You can't wait for the next trip, the next promotion, the bigger house, the next partner. You may be totally uninterested in upsetting your current applecart. I understand that. I was young once and when you are on the upswing your head is filled with dreams and ambitions and the prospect of a future filled with happiness. But life has a way of cruelly thwarting dreams, of seemingly "dealing from the bottom of the deck". For many, that is the time to firmly believe that there is a light at the end of the tunnel of life, that our existence is not just some random occurrence, in the words of Shakespeare, "signifying nothing". But rather, it is a time of growth, a time of enlightenment, a time to prepare for a new beginning.

Depending on where you are on your life's journey you can look back on a series of choices that determined to a very great extent the course of your life and the sum total of what you have achieved during your years of existence. From time to time each of us has the opportunity to engage in what we might call a midterm review. Perhaps each of us could ask ourselves questions like, "How prepared was I to make each of the important decisions in my life?" "Am I happy with myself and where I am going?" "Do I have a good grasp of the meaning of life and my existence?" "What is truth and where does it come from?" "Am I a good person and how do I know that I am good—and what difference does it make anyhow?"

The answers to these questions will be influenced greatly by whether or not we believe in a God Who created us and has put us here on earth for a specific purpose. Thus, we owe it to ourselves to make our choice to believe or not believe with all the knowledge and attention we can bring to bear. There is certainly no lack of information available and there are a myriad of opposing views all competing for your affirmation. So here is my suggestion.

The greatest impediment to making a good choice is our own egotism. Let us assume that you have always been in control and have strong feelings about what you believe and why you do what you do. I challenge you to become humble and make a prayer, as difficult as that may be, and say, "God, if you exist, help me to find you and to understand why you have created me. Help me to seek the good and live as I believe a loving God would want me to live. Help me to trust that you will hear me and let me see the way."

So then what? Try to live as you believe you should live. Seek the Truth. Take some time to evaluate the atheistic arguments. Ask the hard questions. Hold those to account who want to hold sway over you and criticize your wanting to deviate from the accepted norm. Above all, be honest with yourself and keep praying. And when the going gets tough, as it sometimes does, take a moment to look at a starlit sky, behold a newborn babe, listen to an uplifting symphony, cheer a truly noble person and say, "How incomprehensible is the God Who made us and will surely bring us home!"

Chapter Two
God and Truth

Most people have some notion of Who God is and what He is like. The reality is that we can only conjecture and assume because we are in uncharted waters. Theologians and philosophers have reasoned and debated the nature of God for centuries and they have formulated a thesis on the necessary attributes of God—that He is omniscient, all powerful, the source of all that is good and holy, eternal and beyond all human comprehension. He is the source of all Truth, all wisdom, all knowledge. I would like to suggest a framework within which we can relate to God. The first thing we need to do is to avoid trying to make God into our own personal image of what we imagine He is, or should be. Since as noted above, we are limited in making accurate assessments based on our own knowledge we must go to reliable sources to help us understand how to relate to Him in our own lives. The insight from such sources, briefly summarized below, will help us to relate to God within a framework consistent with the best information we have available and with which we can achieve a coherent and motivating purpose in our lives.

God is a spiritual being and in philosophical terms His existence is His essence. What this means is that there is no change in God. There is no activation of some potential capability. For example, a seed planted in fertile soil can become eventually a living plant capable of bearing fruit. This does not happen with God. He is total, complete and perfect now, as He has always been and always will be. When He created the universe, His Divine Intelligence knew everything about all of the created things He made. He knew about the ends for which they were made and willed the good that would result from their achievement of those ends.

The universe is material and as such, must exist in time. Without time there can be no material universe. Time has no meaning in the eternal existence of God. Thus, time came into existence as part of creation and will be in existence only as long as material creation is in existence. Since God is unchanging and has never changed, the act of creation is an eternal act, part of an eternal Divine Plan.

Fundamental to the completion of the Divine Plan is the infinite Wisdom of God which knows all and precedes all and unerringly brings all creation to its final destiny with God in eternity. But only that creation which is inherently eternal will be with God in eternity.

Before going further, it is necessary to speak more about the nature of Truth. Truth may be defined as a fundamental reality, an indisputable fact. It corresponds to the fundamental nature of all created beings and is consistent with the Divine plan of creation. From all eternity God has been the motive force creating and sustaining the universe and ultimately bringing it to completion. The Divine Architect has unerringly directed all within creation toward the fundamental goods for which they were created. The plan created from all eternity, by its very nature, cannot change but will continue under the eternal guidance of God toward its final end. What was true in times past will always be true. What was good in times past must always be good. What was a negation of truth—a deviation from the truth—is still a negation of truth.

A pertinent question is, "Why would God create human beings in the first place?" Our existence adds nothing to His perfection, to His eternal bliss. The only explanation is that He did it out of Love. Love by its very nature seeks not itself, but only the good of another.

Another point to ponder is, "What sort of beings would God create?" Would He create beings which would exist only for a time and then vanish? This would be true in the case of animals which respond to natural instincts and eventually pass from existence. But animals cannot give Him homage, return His love or be with Him eternally. They cannot reason and they cannot will to love.

Human beings have intelligence and free will. They can begin to comprehend the abstract realities of an eternal God; they can make judgments and they can return to God the love He has lavished upon them and seek the perfection that He desires for them. But they can also refuse to love, become caught up in their own egotism and pride, and as a result never achieve the loving perfection for which they were made.

Many have written about how God has influenced their lives, how He has always been there when they needed Him most, especially if they opened their hearts to Him and humbly asked His help. Anyone who earnestly looks at the world around them, with all its magnificence and complexity, must stand in awe at what they comprehend. All creation screams the existence of a loving and providential God Who created all with a plan and a purpose. But what is that purpose?

To help us make an informed decision about whether we can truly believe in God we need to look at what God has made known to us about Himself, things which we could not have determined purely from reason alone. The next chapter will explore how He has communicated to us through His Chosen People and through the promise of a Savior for the human race.

Chapter Three
God Reveals Himself
to His Chosen People

The ancient peoples living in the Fertile Crescent during the second millennium B.C. had no universally accepted moral code and life was filled with violence and rampant immorality. Human life was accorded no innate dignity and the weak were subjugated to the will of the strong. Life had no underlying purpose or meaning.

In the midst of this chaos God called a man named Abram, from the land of Ur, to go to the land of Canaan. There, as the Bible relates in the Book of Genesis, God made with him an eternal covenant. He would be called Abraham and his descendants would be as numerous as the stars in the sky. They would be God's people and He would be their God. *Gen 12:1-3.* Thus began the history of the Jewish People, a history of triumph and tragedy, of a relationship with God Who calls Himself "I Am". By that name God indicated only a present tense, that He does not change, that He cannot change, and that all of His actions are eternal and part of a never-changing divine plan.

Abraham is promised that his wife, Sarah, would bear a son in her old age. His son, Isaac, is born and later fathers his son, Jacob, called Israel, who has twelve sons, the progenitors of the twelve tribes of Israel. The Bible relates how Jacob and his sons, with all their households, migrate to Egypt in a time of famine, but after almost 400 years they are enslaved by the Egyptians. We see in the Book of Exodus in the Bible, how God reveals Himself to Moses in a burning bush. He tells Moses His name and that He has heard the cries of His people under the yoke of bondage by the Egyptians. He instructs Moses to go to Pharaoh and demand that he release the Jews from their servitude. *Ex 2:2-14.* Pharaoh refuses but after suffering through a sequence of ten plagues, the last one resulting in the deaths of all of the first born of the Egyptians, the Pharaoh relents and Moses leads the people out of Egypt to the land promised to them by God in His covenant with Abraham.

God gives them a moral code, the Ten Commandments, and enjoins them through the words of Moses and many prophets through the ages that if they obey His Commandments, they will experience peace and prosperity; but if they do not, He would allow them to fall to the enemies around them and they will no longer have the peace and good fortune they desire.

The first part of the Bible, the Old Testament, relates the astounding history of this people and chronicles their history for almost 2000 years. The book of Genesis, the first book in the Bible, describes the creation of the earth and the first humans, Adam and Eve. As the story unfolds it has similarities to the well-known beliefs of the Semitic people but with a major difference. The Semitic myth relates a tale of chaos verses order, a battleground of the gods. The writer of Genesis, on the other hand, tells of a God outside the turmoil of the Semitic myth, Who creates all and controls all and eliminates all elements of struggle. For a further discussion see *The Two-edged Sword*, pp. 98-102.

Genesis further relates how God made Adam and Eve in His own image with immortal souls. It tells of the disobedience of Adam and Eve in the Garden of Eden when they ate of the fruit of the Tree of Knowledge of Good and Evil and became aware of their sinfulness in the eyes of God. Having lost their innocence, they were banished from the Garden and condemned to a life filled with toil and drudgery. But God promised them a Savior who would atone for their offence and would provide them with a path to eternal bliss.

Scholars tell us that the essential elements we should take from the first part of Genesis is that God created Adam and Eve with immortal souls having intelligence and free will and told them to obey His command to not eat the fruit from the Tree of Knowledge of Good and Evil. God had created them in a state of innocence and they lost that innocence when they disobeyed Him. They also lost any chance to live with God forever, but God told them that He would send a Savior who would bring about their redemption.

For centuries the creation story, that God created the earth and the heavens in six days, was scoffed at by many as a myth. Others accepted it on faith, as fact, but found it difficult to reconcile the words of Genesis with scientific findings over the last several centuries, culminating in today's acceptance of the Big Bang Theory, which, as stated before, places the age of the universe at about 15 billion years. The key point to be made here is that Genesis was never meant in any way to be a scientific document. It was meant to provide a contrasting statement to the myth believed by this ancient people of the time and to show the creative work of the all-powerful God of the Jews.

The recent book, *The Science of God*, pp 43-74, by Gerald Schroeder, referenced earlier, presents the results of a remarkable study that shows that the "days" referred to in Genesis are not the 24-hour days we think of today but are days determined by a "cosmic clock" where the measure of time is dependent on the velocity of the created mass as the universe expanded during the initial stages of the Big Bang. For those who are familiar with concepts of relativity stemming from Albert Einstein's seminal work in the early 20th Century, the book provides a methodology for interpreting Genesis in a way which is both scientifically valid while being faithful to the story presented in Genesis.

The Old Testament presents a history which shows human nature in all its complexity and moral shortcomings. But it also shows a relationship between humanity and a loving God Who repeatedly exhorts His people to follow His decrees but over and over again raises them up after they have corrupted themselves and come to disaster. It is a story of great faith, of treachery, of immorality. But it is also a sublime and uplifting testimony to the presence of Divine guidance which ultimately will bring to fruition the Divine plan to bring forth a Savior to atone for the sin of Adam.

For years many questioned whether the Old Testament stories were true, or were they more in the way of folklore. Beginning in the 19th and 20th Centuries archeological excavations in the regions of the Fertile Crescent found historical records written on stone and on clay tablets, which showed repeatedly that the records of other ancient civilizations living in close proximity to the Jewish nation corroborated the events listed in the Bible. Many of the findings are described in Werner Keller's book, *The Bible as History*. With each new finding there is a gathering consensus in the accuracy of the Bible narrative.

As an example, we have the well-known story of Jacob's second youngest son, Joseph, who is sold by his brothers into slavery in Egypt and through God's help in interpreting Pharaoh's dream of a great famine, is raised to the second in command in the kingdom. It is through Joseph's help that his father and brothers, and their families are brought into Egypt.

The Bible in then silent and after almost 400 years relates that a new Pharaoh ascends to the throne who knew not Joseph. One may wonder what could have caused such a radical change in fortune. The answer is found from the archeological records, as related in Keller's book, pp. 101-121, that show Egypt at the time of Joseph was ruled by the Hyksos, Asiatic people who had overrun Egypt and remained in control for over 150 years. The Egyptians eventually regained control and looked down upon the foreigners who had emigrated from the Fertile Crescent years before during the time of Joseph and had overrun their country. They put heavy restrictions upon them and eventually made them slaves to perform the menial building tasks to further the new pharaoh's building projects.

The history of Israel in the Promised Land is initially one of conquest, establishing supremacy among neighboring nations in the Fertile Crescent. Under the leadership of King David, the nation enters a period of great success, culminating during the reign of King David's son, Solomon. Solomon builds a temple to God in Jerusalem and becomes the greatest and most wise monarch of his time.

But he succumbs to the wishes of his many wives and offers sacrifice to their pagan gods. In punishment, God decrees that Solomon's kingdom will be divided after his reign. Solomon's son, Rehoboam, becomes the ruler of only the tribes of Judah and Benjamin in Jerusalem, with the other 10 tribes establishing their own kingdom in the north.

Then ensues a period of apostasy and disobedience to God's commandments culminating in destruction of the northern kingdom by the Assyrians in 724 BC and the forcible transfer of the people to Assyria. As part of the same military campaign the Assyrian king, Sennacherib, laid siege to Jerusalem and demanded surrender of the city. King Hezekiah of Judah, refused, relying on the words of the prophet, Isaiah,

> *Thus says the Lord concerning the King of Assyria: he shall not come into this city or shoot an arrow there, or come with a shield or set up a siege mound against it. By the way he came by the same way he shall return. He shall not enter the city. Isa 37: 33-35.*

The next day Sennacherib did depart with no explanation given in the Assyrian records. But an Egyptian force which had come to defend their northern border told of a great disaster which befell the Assyrians resulting in the deaths of thousands, which the records showed as the occurrence of a plague which decimated Sennacherib's army and forced him to retreat to Nineveh. Again I reference Keller's book, pp. 298-302.

In 587 BC Jerusalem does fall to the army of Nebuchadnezzar of Babylon and most of the inhabitants are carried away to Babylon. The prophet, Jeremiah, repeatedly pleaded with the leaders of Jerusalem to trust in God and that He would deliver them from defeat. But they insisted on relying on an alliance with Egypt to protect them. They also had come to the belief that God had ordained that Jerusalem would never fall to invaders, no matter what they did.

Even at this low point in the history of His chosen people God promises that after 70 years He will bring His people back to Jerusalem and promises to renew His covenant with them, the covenant He established with Abraham, and confirmed though Moses and David, that the Messiah will come from the house of David.

It is at this time of great sorrow and destruction, as the Bible relates, God, through the words of His prophet, Jeremiah, declares His intent to establish a new covenant, but it would be different:

> *Behold the days are coming, declares the Lord, when I will make a new covenant with the house of Israel, and the house of Judah, not like the covenant I made with their fathers on the day when I took them out of Egypt, my covenant that they broke, though I was their husband, declares the Lord. For this is the covenant that I will make with the house of Israel after those days, declares the Lord: I will put my law within them, and I will write it on their hearts. And I will be their God and they will be my people. And no longer will each one teach his neighbor and each his brother, saying, "Know the Lord," for they shall all know me, from the least of them to the greatest, declares the Lord. For I will forgive their iniquity and remember their sin no more. Jer 31:31-34.*

The days of Babylon were numbered and the Kingdom of Persia conquered Babylon. Cyrus, a just king, becomes supreme in the entire region. Then, according to the Bible, God is shown to begin His accomplishment of the words of Jeremiah: "In the first year of Cyrus, King of Persia, in order to fulfill the word of the Lord spoken by Jeremiah, the Lord inspired King Cyrus of Persia to issue this proclamation throughout his kingdom by word of mouth and in writing:

> *Thus says Cyrus, King of Persia: All the kingdoms of the earth the Lord the God of heaven has given to me and he also charged me to build him a house in Jerusalem, which is in Judah. Whoever, therefore among you who belongs to any part of his people, let him go up and may his God be with him." 2 Chron 38:22-23.*

In the year 537 BC, the remnant of those carried away to Babylon returned to Jerusalem bringing back precious jewels taken from Solomon's temple and freely given back to them by Cyrus. During the following years the temple was rebuilt and expectation began to build that the promised Messiah would come, announced in the words of the Prophet Malachi:

> *Lo, I am sending my messenger to prepare the way before me, and suddenly there will come to the temple the Lord whom you seek, and the messenger*

of the covenant whom you desire. Yes, he is coming,
says the Lord of hosts. But who will endure the day
of his coming and who can stand when he appears?
For he is like a refiner's fire ... and he will purify
the sons of Levi. Mal 3:1-3.

In the fullness of time a man does appear, claiming to be the promised Messiah, but claiming more—to be the Son of God.

Chapter Four
Jesus Christ

What do you know about Jesus Christ? If you are like most adults you have heard about him, can cite some of the things he did and maybe you have accepted him as your Lord and Savior. If asked more specific information—

> E.g., What proof do we have that he really lived and was crucified? Why do you think it is reasonable to believe that he rose from the dead? Is he the Son of God, equal to and one in being with the Father?

—what would you reply?

Before providing more insight into the answers to the above questions, why should this be especially important? I have just introduced in the previous chapter, in somewhat general terms, a basic understanding of the nature of God and Truth. I said that we can conclude only a limited amount about God because without direct revelation we are limited in our knowledge.

In the previous chapter I presented evidence that God indeed intervened in our existence. I traced the history of the Jewish people, chosen by God to be His people and to bring forth a Savior who would atone for the sin of Adam and Eve, our first parents. Now we have in the person of Jesus Christ one who claims to be God and the promised Messiah. He has taught as one in authority the purpose of our existence and God's plan for our salvation. If Jesus is who he says he is, then his words are of the utmost importance because they speak the truth of our existence and we had best learn and understand what he said and why we should believe it.

From the perspective of many, Jesus Christ is the most important figure in all of human history. In a small but meaningful way the separation of two periods of history into that before Christ, BC, and that after Christ, AD, is especially noteworthy. How can one man have achieved so much? The answer for many is very simple. He is the Son of God.

Reading what I just wrote one might have assumed that he came in glory and presented himself to the world in great power and majesty. But he came in poverty, known to only a few, and while he was a baby, Herod, the king of Judea, tried to kill him in a vain attempt to prevent him from becoming the king he was meant to be. He lived in obscurity for 30 years and then appeared and the world changed forever. Perhaps the best way to more fully understand what happened is to read an excerpt from the writings of Josephus, a famous Jewish historian of the time. The passage is taken from the Slavonic (Old Russian) translation of the Jewish War, referenced by

Warren Carroll in his book, *The Founding of Christendom*, pp 296-297. Josephus describes the scene vividly:

> *It was at this time that a man appeared-if "man" is the right word—who had all of the attributes of a man but seemed to be something greater. His actions, certainly, were superhuman, for he worked such wonderful and amazing miracles that I for one cannot regard him as a man. But in view of his likeness to ourselves I cannot regard him as an angel either. Everything that some hidden power enabled him to do he did by an authoritative word. ... Many of the common people flocked after him and followed his teaching ... When the crowds grew bigger he earned by his actions an incomparable reputation. The exponents of the Law were mad with jealousy and gave Pilate 30 talents to have him executed ... It is also stated that after his execution he disappeared entirely. Some people assert he had risen; others retort his friends had stolen him away. I for one cannot decide where the truth lies. A dead man cannot rise by his own power, but he might rise if aided by the prayer of another righteous man. Again, if an angel or some other heavenly being, or God himself takes human form to fulfill His purpose, and after living among men, dies and is buried, He can then rise again at will. Moreover, it is stated that he could not have been stolen away, as*

guards were placed around his tomb, 30 Romans and 1000 Jews.

Josephus' writing documents that Jesus did live, was crucified and then by the testimony of many, rose from the dead. One may wonder how credible is the testimony of the many, but their ensuing actions speak louder than their words. Tradition tells us that all but one of Jesus' closest followers, his apostles, suffered agonizing deaths because of their preaching, never denying what they witnessed and believed concerning their Lord and Master. The apostle, John, was miraculously saved from death in a cauldron of boiling oil and was the one apostle who died a natural death.

The most astounding claim that Jesus made during his public life was that he is the Son of God, the Second Person of the Triune Godhead. He repeatedly urged His listeners to let the truth of what he said be proven by his works, his miracles. The leaders of the Jews would not accept what he said and condemned him to death for blasphemy—making himself, a man, equal to God. His apostles were devastated by his death, but on the third day his tomb was found empty and his followers claimed to have seen him in a risen body which was not constrained by time and space and could appear in human flesh at any time and then just as quickly disappear.

Jesus was seen repeatedly over a period of 40 days and was then seen to ascend into the heavens. Shortly after

Jesus' ascension into heaven the apostles experienced a miraculous change when they were filled with the Spirit of God and became totally changed. Men who had been simple, uneducated followers, became fearless preachers of the teachings Jesus gave them, first to the Jews, and then to the furthest reaches of the known world, fulfilling Jesus' command to teach all nations, baptizing them in the name of the Father and of the Son and of the Holy Spirit, and to establish his Church. The travels of the leader of the apostles, Peter, as well as John, the Evangelist, are well known within the confines of the Roman Empire. Other apostles traveled to other lands, never controlled by Rome. Andrew went to what it now Ukraine; Philip, to Asia Minor; Thaddaeus Jude, to Mesopotamia; Simon, to Persia; and Thomas, to India.

In fulfillment of Jesus' command, the apostles worked tirelessly to build His Church, suffering through many persecutions, remaining true to their calling, and transforming the world. They provided the means for His followers to achieve their prime purpose in life, to work toward their salvation and achieve everlasting life with God. They wrote gospel narratives documenting what Jesus taught and did, the miracles he performed, his passion, his crucifixion and his resurrection from the dead. All of the gospels, a record of the ensuing work of the apostles after Jesus returned to heaven, and instructive letters to the various Christian communities established by the apostles are all contained in the New Testament of the Bible.

The composite of both the Old and New Testaments provides a unity of salvation history, encapsulating God's continuous guidance to His chosen people through the period of the Old Testament, preparing them through the repeated words of the prophets for the coming of the promised Messiah. In the New Testament Jesus is shown as fulfilling all of the prophecies concerning the Messiah and bringing to fruition the Divine Plan for salvation of the human race. In his book, *Messiah in Both Testaments*, Fred John Meldau presents this incisive quote from British pastor D. M. Paston:

> *The most amazing drama that ever was presented to the mind of man—a drama written in prophesy in the Old Testament and in biography in the four gospels of the New Testament—is the narrative of Jesus, the Christ. One outstanding fact, among many, completely isolates Him. It is this: this one man only in the history of the world has had explicit details given beforehand of His birth, life, death and resurrection; that these details are given in documents given to the public centuries before He appeared, and that no one challenges, or can challenge that these documents were widely circulated long before His birth, and that anyone and everyone can compare for himself or herself the actual records of His life, with those ancient documents, and find that they match one another perfectly.*

For those who want to explore in more detail the prophecies and the precursors in the Old Testament and how they relate in totality to the fulfillment related in the New Testament, the book, *The Emmaus Code*, by David Limbaugh presents a fascinating and detailed exposition. The New Covenant referred to by God in the quote from Jeremiah, given above, is established through the sacrifice of His only begotten Son, Jesus, in atonement for the sins of men. The sacrifice of animals in the Old Testament is replaced by that of Jesus on the Cross and the fruit of His sacrifice is available to all who believe in Him and follow in His footsteps along the path of love of God and love of neighbor.

Jesus' passion and death on the cross were very difficult for many of the Jews to accept. They expected a triumphant Messiah who would establish his kingdom on earth and free the Jews from domination by Rome. They did not comprehend the meaning of the passage from Isaiah that clearly foretold what would occur:

> *He was spurned and avoided by men, a man of suffering, accustomed to infirmity, one of those from whom men hide their faces—yet it was our infirmities that he bore, our sufferings that he endured.—Like a lamb led to the slaughter, or a sheep before the shearers, he was silent and opened not his mouth. Oppressed and condemned, he was taken away, and who would have thought any more*

of his destiny? When he was cut off from the land of the living and smitten for the sin of his people a grave was assigned him among the wicked and a burial place with evildoers though he had done no wrong.—Because of his affliction he shall see the light in fulness of days. Through his suffering, my servant shall justify many and their guilt he shall bear. Isa 53:3;4;7-9;13.

Indicative of God's continuing action, He chose Paul, the Apostle to the Gentiles, to bring the news of salvation first to the Jews, and then to the gentiles. This was in accordance with His words to Abraham in His covenant with him, "and in your descendants all of the nations of the earth will find blessing". *Gen 22:18.*

This was the same one, then called Saul, who mercilessly persecuted the early believers and stood in witness of the stoning to death of Stephen, the first one martyred for his belief in Jesus. Paul was later blinded by a heavenly light on his way from Jerusalem to Damascus and heard a voice of Jesus asking him "Saul, Saul, why are you persecuting me?" He replied, "Who are you, Sir." The reply came, "I am Jesus, whom you are persecuting. Now get up and go into the city and you will be told what to do." *Acts 9:4-6. He* was led by his companions to Damascus where, Ananias, a disciple of Jesus, cured his blindness and baptized him. He later began his missionary travels, preaching first to the Jews and then to the gentiles,

the gospel message. He would maintain contact with the
congregations of believers that he established by sending
them letters addressing their concerns and questions and
continuing his instructions to them. These letters later
were incorporated into the New Testament.

The record of Paul's travels and teachings supplement
the message of the gospels and show a depth of knowledge
and wisdom which could only have come from Divine
Revelation. Paul describes his experience in which he "was
caught up into Paradise and heard ineffable things that no
one can utter." *2 Cor 12:1-5.* The sublimity of his teachings, complementing as they do the gospel narratives,
leaves little doubt as to the work of the Divine Architect to
rise up leaders to do His work in the grand plan of
salvation.

To summarize, if Jesus is who he says he is, then by his
own words he brings to us the Truth of the living God
Who created us and presents to us the path to eternal life.
St. Paul writes in his First Epistle to the Corinthians, "If
Christ be not risen from the dead then our religion is in
vain and we are still mired in our sins." *1 Cor 8:14.* Those
who claim that Jesus was just another good man who
taught ideals that men can use to help them live better
lives, have no basis for what they allege. A "good man"
who claims something which is not true is a liar. God
could not have been with him and he could not have
performed the miracles that he did. Most importantly he
could not have risen from the dead.

Those who claim that he did not rise from the dead must then explain the empty tomb, guarded by soldiers, who later claimed that the apostles stole the body from the tomb while they were asleep. This story was derisively scorned by Jesus followers, who all testified by their actions and painful deaths that they had seen Jesus alive after his crucifixion and never wavered in their conviction.

The next chapter recounts the history of the church established by the apostles, the Roman Catholic Church.

Chapter Five
The One, Holy, Catholic and Apostolic Church

What do you know about the Catholic Church? Perhaps you were raised catholic and drifted away. Perhaps you heard about the Church at some point but were never really familiar with its history and claim to be the true church established by Jesus' apostles. The record is clear and irrefutable. The Catholic Church is the Church established by the apostles. The early Christians worshiped, taught and believed in accordance with what was taught by the apostles and that same belief and worship is existent in the Catholic Church. Central to that worship is the holy sacrifice of the Mass where the priest, through the power given by Jesus to His apostles the night before he died on the cross, changes the bread and wine of the sacrifice into the body and blood of Christ. This sacrifice is the renewal of Jesus' sacrifice on the Cross for our salvation, and the communion received by the faithful is the body and blood of Christ.

This is in accordance with the words of Jesus from the Gospel of John in the New Testament, "Amen, amen, I say to you, unless you eat of the flesh of the Son of Man and drink his blood you shall not have life within you.

Whoever eats this bread and drinks this blood has life everlasting and I will raise him up on the last day." *Jn 6:54. Many* of his followers, when they heard these words, found it to be a "hard saying" and followed him no longer.

But His apostles and many of His followers did believe Him. They saw the miracles Jesus performed and believed that the God of their fathers Who led them out of Egypt, brought them to the promised land and made them His people, the God Who created the universe and sent His only begotten Son to redeem them, could do all things. In philosophical terms, the accidents (appearances we see) are bread and wine, but the substance (reality that is contained) is changed from bread and wine into the body and blood of Jesus.

As one looking out from the inside, I am continually amazed as I hear others refer to the Catholic Church. The embedded notions and conclusions about the Church have been passed down for centuries and provide an undercurrent of distrust and suspicion which never seem to materially subside. Like so many beliefs in the common consciousness of today's culture their sources are specious at best and once enunciated they become like granite pillars of accepted fact never again to stand exposed in the light of day.

From the earliest period of its existence the Church has withstood attacks from outside. During its first three centuries Rome, with all its power, tried repeatedly to exterminate a belief which it found objectionable, and persecuted those unwilling to offer sacrifice to Roman gods.

During those centuries there were 10 major persecutions resulting in martyrdom for thousands of Christians.

In the year 312 Caesar Constantine defeated Caesar Maxentius, who controlled Rome, in a decisive battle on the banks of the Tiber River and became the undisputed Emperor of Rome. Prior to the battle Constantine had a vision of a cross in the sky and the words, "With this sign, you will conquer." Constantine had the sign of the cross placed on the shields of all of his soldiers. After the battle Constantine rode in victory before the welcoming crowds of Rome. Ref: *The Founding of Christendom*, pp. 528-530.

With the coming of Constantine, the Church became the official Church of the Roman Empire and its fortunes changed enormously. It was no longer a crime to be a Christian, as it had been for over 250 years. The Church gained a powerful voice in the political and religious affairs of the empire, but it still had the primary responsibility to remain true to the teachings of its founder, Jesus Christ.

The work of the Church through the centuries following its emergence from the catacombs of Rome was central to the development of the civilized world of Europe and the surrounding area, especially during the Dark Ages when the onslaught of the barbarian invasions caused repeated and catastrophic misery and destruction.

With the rise of Islam in the middle of the 7th century Christianity and Islam embarked on a titanic struggle for the control of Europe, North Africa, and the Middle East. The followers of the Prophet, Mohamed, spread their new religion by conquest and colonization. Inhabitants were given the choice of converting to Islam, or paying a tax and becoming subject to the rule of the Islamic state. By the end of the 11th century Islamic control extended from Asia Minor through all of Northern Africa and over about half of Spain and Portugal. From early in the 8th century, when Muslim control extended over all of Spain and Portugal, except for a small mountainous region in the northwest corner of Spain, there had been a never-ending war of re-conquest by the Spanish to regain control of all of the Iberian Peninsula. By the end of the 11th century the long war was only half over. I here reference two books, *The Middle East,* and the second and third volumes of Warren Carroll's history of Christendom, *The Building of Christendom* and *The Glory of Christendom.*

It was at this time that cries from Christians in the Holy Land, controlled by Islam for over 400 years, reached Rome and initiated a call from Pope Urban II to launch a crusade to free the Holy Land from the control of the Muslims. The result of the First Crusade, launched by European knights and foot-soldiers, was a recapture of the Holy Land and the return of control to the Christians, The Christian control lasted for almost 100 years, when the Muslims again regained control. Later crusades, extending into the 13th century tried repeatedly to regain control of the Holy land, but without success.

However, the war between Islam and Christianity did not abate. The battle line extending from the Middle East to the Atlantic Ocean astride the Mediterranean Sea carried on through the next four centuries, encompassing the fall of Constantinople to the forces of the Sultan, Mehmet, in 1453, and the ensuing battle for the control of the Mediterranean Sea, which lasted until almost the end of the 16th century. During this period there were titanic battles for control of the Islands of Rhodes, Malta and Crete, and a final sea battle, Lepanto, which would end most major Islamic-Christians confrontations. See the book, *Empires of the Sea,* for a riveting description of this violent period. After the battle of Lepanto both sides came to the realization that neither could dominate and there ensued a period of uneasy peace. The concomitant rise of the major European powers during the ensuing centuries changed the armed struggles from religious to nationalistic.

The leaders of the Church were also beset with a never-ending task of trying to control the actions of tyrannical emperors and kings through the power of the Church to excommunicate those who would not obey laws and norms of conduct. In extreme cases the Pope could impose interdict on cities or entire countries, curtailing religious observances and allowing subjects to renounce their allegiances to the leader so punished. Often this resulted in armed interventions aimed directly at the Pope and the control of the Papal States, ruled by the Pope. More than once the Pope was caused to flee for his life and other times was kept in captivity.

One of the most pervasive and recurring problems for the Church from the earliest years of its existence was the condemnation and eradication of heresies—contradictions to the core beliefs of the Faith, promulgated by would-be teachers of new doctrine based upon individual determinations of what they believed to be the truth. In some cases, these were teachings promulgated for personal gain, as in the case of Simon Magus, in Samaria, during the time of Peter, the leader of the apostles, and the first Pope. Simon asked Peter to give to him the secret of the miracles that he performed, to which Peter responded, "May your money perish with you because you thought you could buy the gift of God with money." *Act 9:20,* Simon was a magician who tried to convince others that he was a god.

During the first several centuries false teachings continued to be introduced, denying core elements of the teachings of Christ. Manes claimed that there are two gods, one good and one evil. This claim gave rise to the Manichean Heresy. Arius later claimed that Christ is not equal to the Father and that at some point did not exist. The Montanists championed an austere regimen of conduct that denigrated marriage and encouraged adherents to adhere to extreme rules of conduct.

One of the most dangerous heresies was Gnosticism, which, among many other erroneous principles (such as salvation by secret knowledge), identified the flesh as inherently evil. Only the spirit was deemed good. From time to time this Gnostic belief would reappear, sometimes in an extremely virulent form. In the early Middle Ages, in southern France, the sect, known as the Cathars, proclaimed that all earthly life, marriage and the bearing of children were inherently evil, that salvation could only be obtained through the efforts of those, called "The Perfect," who could deliver to those on their deathbeds, the Consolamentum, which included a specific renunciation of the Church and the Cross. The sect took a firm hold and large numbers were attracted to it. Violence erupted, the Church felt obliged to eradicate a belief which endangered the souls of Christians and championed suicide, encouraging the murder of anyone, who having received the Consolamentum, then recovered from their illness.

Many leaders of the Church gave their lives for the Faith and have been elevated to Sainthood. Unfortunately, there were others who succumbed to worldly desires and disgraced their calling. We must remember that Jesus promised only that He, through the ongoing guidance of the Holy Spirit, would keep the Church free from error in proclaiming the message of the Gospel. He did not guarantee that all of his hierarchy would be faithful to His decrees. Many of them were not. But He promised that the gates of hell would not prevail against His Church and that it would never cease to exist.

In our own time, incidents of sexual abuse by members of the clergy have caused great pain and disillusionment and have caused many to leave the Church. The great tragedy is that those who have left no longer participate in the life-giving worship and prayer of the Church. They fixate on the moral shortcomings of a few and equate those to a shortcoming in the Church Jesus established. Do they not realize that Jesus predicted that there would be false teachers, that there would be dissension, but that the guidance of the Holy Spirit would always be there? That in God's own due time He would raise up leaders, as in the time of St. Francis, who would rebuild His Church.

The early 13th Century was a time of decline in the Church and many leaders were overly involved with earthly matters and neglected the spiritual welfare of their people. Like in our own times, the result was a decrease in the love and devotion to God and the Faith. Warren Carroll in the third volume of his comprehensive history of Christendom, *The Glory of Christendom*, p. 159, sums up the situation concisely:

> *One of the greatest paradoxes in the spiritual history of humanity—and an essential element in the mystery of the Cross—is that prosperity of any kind tends to draw men away from God. The poor keep the Faith when the rich apostatize. The dark ages are ages of faith, while progress brings doubt and even scorn toward the Truth which is God's and the God Who is Truth.*

Francis was from a rich family and responded to God's call to rebuild the Church. He gathered together a group of followers who forsook the things of this world to work among the poor. Francis established the Friars Minor and with his companions worked incessantly to draw souls to Christ. I draw again from the words of Warren Carroll: Ibid, p. 206-207.

> *No mortal man upon this earth—still less a mere historian—can guess the magnitude of the blessings St. Francis of Assisi brought to mankind by his prayer and intercession during the twenty years when he knew and fulfilled his mission on earth. But we surely cannot go far wrong if we see many of those blessings of Christendom that flowered as never before or since in the fifty years that followed his death.*

Those who may have chosen to leave the Church should remember that the Church is still the eternal source of Truth and the necessary means for Her children to work out their salvation. The actions of a few do not destroy the essence of the Church promised by Jesus to be guided by the Holy Spirit and to endure until the end of time. Often during the last two millennia there have been faulty shepherds of the faithful who have debased themselves and caused great pain. We live in a hostile world which can corrupt even those chosen by God to lead His Church.

What then is needed in these difficult times is faithfulness, prayer and the firm belief that God will always provide a way, will always provide the grace, and that in the end, good will triumph over evil. To leave the Church in such times is to shirk one's duty to evangelize and spread the good news of the gospel and to deny oneself the sustenance and the many life-giving graces which can provide solace and renewed hope.

Many will try now, as others have tried in the past, to bring about the demise of the Church, to no avail. It was the blood of the martyrs which provided the impetus for the Church's emergence during the many Roman persecutions and that impetus was no less felt during the many persecutions in our own era. The wellspring of Faith and the unquenchable hope in eternal life will never be extinguished by the blandishments and promises of a secular world.

Yet the world still tries to look for its own way. It sees suffering, injustice and a society driven by personal gain and an aversion to any kind of restraint on conduct. When those in the Church stumble and betray the trust placed in them it is not looked upon as only personal sin but as a failure of the institution itself. As Pope Benedict XVI, in his encyclical *"Saved by Hope"*, *Par. 30*, described it, the world seeks to establish the kingdom of man led by science and politics to replace the failed Kingdom of God which did not establish the perfect world anticipated by the champions of "Enlightenment", beginning in the 18th Century and continuing to our present day.

We see the results of such efforts in the wars, the pogroms and the never-ending conflicts. Man's fallen nature cannot be cured by manmade remedies and wishful dreams of what should have been. It can only be addressed by a return to the path of love proclaimed by Jesus and carried forth by his disciples and all those who tread along the path of righteousness. But many will say that "It has not worked. It is too hard." It has not worked because it has not been earnestly believed and has not been fully attempted.

Jesus foreknew the result. Did He not say that the cross would always be a part of our lives? *Mk 8:34.* Will we ever have paradise on earth? We will have paradise in heaven. Why should we try when we know we cannot succeed? We are tasked to try, to evangelize and to reside in hope—hope that in His own time God will prevail; the firm belief that in His Wisdom God has chosen the better way.

From the inside of the Church community, committed believers, and there are many, carry on their devotions daily amidst the din of modern-day life. They are not oblivious to the external upheavals. They hurt and are seriously troubled when those within the Church fail to live up to their call for holiness and service. They do not appreciate being made the object of derision and false accusations frequently leveled by many who claim to be proponents of love and goodness but their actions speak otherwise. Yet deep within them is a serenity and an understanding. The follower is not superior to his Master. Jesus predicted that there would be conflicts and persecutions just because of Him. They subscribe to the firm belief that His Kingdom is not here and that He will be with them always until they arrive in their eternal home.

Those who have delved into Church history have found that the Church, since its founding, has been central to the history of humanity. Untold numbers have trod its paths of faith and service. The message has always been the same. Share the good news! Preach the Word, in season and out of season! Do not teach what has not been given. And in the words of Jesus, "This is my commandment, love one another as I have loved you." *Jn 15:12;* "If you love me, you will keep my commandments." *Jn 15:14.*

The work of the Church in ministering to the poor and downtrodden is beyond compare. Her missionaries give their lives in foreign lands to preach the word and help those in need. They do this in response to Christ's call to feed the hungry, give drink to the thirsty, clothe the naked...enunciated in *Mt 25.* They do this in accordance with Paul's message to the Corinthians to help with the collection being made for the needy in Jerusalem, "Now as you excel in every respect, in faith, discourse, knowledge, all earnestness, and in the love we have for you, may you excel in this generous act also". *2 Cor 8:7.*

And what of the beauty and profound wisdom which has flowed from the works of thousands of artisans, poets, composers, intellectuals, scientists, and scholars. What of the company of the Saints which have followed the Way and achieved their rewards. What of the liturgy and the sublimity of the worship that unceasingly rises to God from all corners of the world declaring that Jesus is Lord!

And yet the naysayers abound. "The Church went astray sometime after the first centuries of Christianity. The reformers of the 16th Century found the true way." How can that be when the dogma and liturgy and teaching of the Catholic Church are the same as that practiced by early Christians? The Didache, the catechism of the early Church dates from the First Century. The teachings in the Didache on the essential precepts of the Faith, the sacraments, the liturgy, Church organization and moral imperatives are those of the Catholic Church. *Clement of Rome, The Didache, pp. 57-77.* A later exposition of the essential elements of the Church written by Justin Martyr to Roman Emperor, Antonius Pius, in the Second Century delineates in unmistakable clarity the same essential elements of today's Catholic Church. *The Four Witnesses,* pp. 177-198.

"Catholics worship Mary." I have been a faithful Catholic for many decades and I have *never* heard a Catholic say that Mary is divine or equal to God. The Church has always taught that Mary shows us the way to Jesus and is central to God's plan of salvation. Many other faiths treat her like an extra in a movie who bears Jesus, the Son of God, in her womb and then just goes off the stage until the next commemoration of Christmas. Rather, she is lauded like Judith, in the Book of Judith in the Old Testament (Catholic Bible), "You are the glory of Jerusalem, the surpassing joy of Israel. You are the splendid boast of our people." *Jth 15:9.* It is these words which the Church applies to Mary in honor of her complete submission to the will of the Father and her preeminent position as the Mother of the King.

Ask any question about the Church's teachings. Investigate any historical incident. Carefully research the lives of the many saints and martyrs. You will find answers and detailed expositions on faith, morals, theology, and philosophy. You will find historical records, early copies of the gospels, letters, copies of early versions of the Old Testament, deliberations of the Church Councils, the work of formulating the books of Scripture that comprise our Bible. Many who hold to the words of Scripture as the only source of what is to be believed deny the importance of Tradition, as indicated by St. Paul in his Second Epistle to the Thessalonians, "Therefore, brothers, stand firm and hold fast to the traditions you were taught, either by an oral statement or by a letter of ours." 2 *Thes 2:15*.

In the year 393 a synod of bishops meeting in Africa specified the complete list of books of the Bible, those deemed to be divinely inspired. The list was approved by Pope Innocent in 405. This was the first time that a definitive statement of what books would constitute the accepted Scripture of the Church. Those who hold to Sola Scriptura never seem to understand that it is because of the Church that we have the Scripture available to us today.

One of the Church Fathers, Tertullian of Carthage, wrote in the Second Century arguing against those who would privately interpret Scripture, *The Four Witnesses*, pp 158-159:

In order that we may be judged to have the truth—
we who walk in the rule which the churches have
handed down from the apostles, the apostles from
Christ, and Christ from God—admit that the
reasonableness of our position is clear, that heretics
should not be allowed to challenge us by an appeal
to the Scriptures, since we, without using Scripture,
prove they have nothing to do with Scripture. If they
are heretics, they cannot be Christians, because it is
not from Christ that they have gotten what they
pursue of their own choosing, and from which they
incur the name heretic.

In an age of denial and societal upheaval, when many seek some harbor from the storm, how blessed it is to find an oasis of belief and beauty, built on rock and promised to last forever. This is what is promised to true believers who hear the Word of God and rejoice in its meaning, and who remember the words of their Lord, "I am with you always until the end of time." *Mt 28:20.*

In the next chapter we will trace the reasons why the Church established by the apostles became fractured, resulting in the vast multitude of churches all claiming to teach what Jesus taught, but differing radically in the message they teach.

Chapter Six
Which Christianity

Do you actively belong to a church? Did you ever wonder how so many churches can believe contradictory things, yet maintain that they are all faithful to the teachings of Christ?

"I pray not only for them but also for those who will believe in me through their word so that they will all be one." *Jn 18,20.* In these words to His disciples just before His passion and death Jesus prayed to the Father for unity for all His followers. How well we see today the need for that unity! We see, even in our own country, thousands of separate churches claiming to teach in the name of Jesus. Many teachings are contradictory and many followers maintain strong views on what they will or will not believe. How can anyone searching for what Jesus actually taught be confident that what he hears preached to him is true?

As discussed earlier, Truth is eternal and unchanging and is the essence of the Godhead from which it came. It is not subject to the opinion or evolving understanding of men. It is the reason why Jesus came into the world, as He told Pilate at his trial, "I came to give testimony to the Truth." *Jn 18:37.*

For a number of years different denominations have gathered together to join in services stressing those areas of belief in which they are in agreement. But to strive for unity what is required is an in-depth discussion of what separates them. When did the differences begin and what are reasons they began? How do the various beliefs relate to the available sources that define what Jesus actually taught and was later promulgated by his apostles? The information is available. What is required is for people of good will to diligently seek the truth.

How did all of the chaos come about? It was not present during the early centuries of Christianity. As discussed earlier, there were heresies—a number described earlier, regarding largely theological understanding of Who Jesus is, the sources of good and evil, and the nature and authority of the Church He established. But there was unity under one creed and one vicar of Christ, the pope.

In the 11th Century the Eastern (Orthodox) Churches separated from the Church in Rome. The Dogmas preached by the apostles were held by both Churches, except that the Orthodox Churches no longer accepted the leadership of the Roman pontiff. They would not accept that Jesus, in His declaration to Peter, "Thou art Peter and upon this rock I will build my Church and the gates of hell will not prevail against it. And I will give to you the keys to the kingdom. What you shall bind on earth will be bound also in heaven and what you shall loose on earth shall also be loosed in heaven", *Mt 16:16-19*, was establishing under the leadership of Peter and his successors the primacy of teaching authority that would maintain the consistency and accuracy of taught doctrine for all ages.

This situation was maintained until the time of the Protestant Reformation which began in 1517, led by Martin Luther. During a period of almost 500 years the Faith believed by the vast majority of Christians was the same even though the schism between the eastern and western branches of Christianity remained.

In the 15th and 16th Centuries the Church leaders grew lax in their observance of the moral truths they claimed to profess. The Church came under attack by Martin Luther, John Calvin and others in a number of areas concerning Church doctrines. The ensuing disputes quickly escalated into outright ruptures and large groups of Christians separated from unity with Rome and established their own churches. The weakened authority and the need for reform within the Church prevented any healing of the breach. Once separated from a central authority these new religious groups began to evolve their own doctrines of belief, claiming that they were free to interpret Scripture on their own without leadership from Rome. But on whose authority were they making these changes?

The Council of Trent made reforms in Church organization and eliminated the taking of money for the granting of indulgences, loudly condemned by Luther within his famous ninety-five theses nailed to the Wittenberg palace wall in October, 1517. But it was too late. The breech had begun and it was destined to proceed and fester for centuries.

May God grant that all who believe in Jesus and seek to follow His way will find peace and strength to stand firm against a world which seeks only to follow the easy way, to make up its own rules and abide by its own creed. Each person must walk sincerely in the way of truth, without equivocation and without succumbing to selfishness and pride. For some, the way of their birth or the result of their honest determination has defined a path which is right for them. For others, the way may be less clear and they may be still searching.

I appeal to those in the last group, who lack something to believe in. They may have previously belonged to some denomination or group and have left due to doctrinal disagreements, the leadership in their particular congregation or for any of a number of reasons. When they find a new affiliation, it is usually a hit or miss attempt to satisfy their need to belong to some faith community.

If one really wanted to find out who Jesus actually was, what he taught, what church he established and where that church is today, the information is readily available. But it will take effort. One cannot just randomly join different congregations and pick one that seems friendly and right and let it go at that. Many do that and perhaps achieve some peace of mind, but others will continue to question and look for answers to the same issues of truth raised above.

It seems quite reasonable and clearly obvious that to find the real Jesus we must go back to where it all started. In previous chapters I have discussed what we know about Jesus and His church established by his apostles. I have discussed the history of that church, the Catholic Church, and have presented evidence that proves it is the true church, teaching what Jesus taught. Some readers may want to delve further into these topics and there is no lack of information available. The only limitation will be the sincerity of those who search for the Truth. Many have previously traveled the same path. The more they learned the more they became encouraged to investigate further.

Most will have some starting point based on their upbringing and life experience. Perhaps the church they originally attended did not meet their needs, or became less and less important to the life they wanted to lead. In many cases they may have had a shallow exposure to the faith of their birth and left it not because of its shortcomings but due to the way it was perceived. But fundamentally each searcher should ask his or her self, "Why is this important to me? Am I willing to diligently search for the Truth? Am I willing to do what will be required when I find the Truth?"

There are also many who just want to maintain a rather tenuous relationship with some religious community.

There are frequently issues concerning baptism, marriage, funeral rites and some latent desire to belong to something. As I once heard it put, "They want an insurance policy, just in case they may need it for whatever may come in their future lives." They are the ones who show up on the big days—Christmas, Easter—and are then seldom seen again until the next year. Perhaps they assume that if they attend a few times a year and believe, that they will be considered to be fully enrolled members.

How is a person's peace of mind or happiness related to their faith and contentment in what they are achieving? People who have no strong beliefs that define who they are can become driven by whimsical winds of change that control their every action. They seek only what seems good for themselves and give little heed to the consequences. Many who start off this way, seeing that they are floundering, look for some stability and meaning in their lives. Thus they frequently look to religion or to other sources to relieve the anxiety which they are feeling.

If one is in this state of anxiety or has established no basic plan or basis for their life, all of their subsequent actions and choices are on uncertain foundations. The result can be making decisions with inadequate foreknowledge of what can be expected. When difficulties arise, as they frequently do, they make new choices and the results may differ little from those obtained before because the same inadequate knowledge and preparation persist.

From a theological perspective what is ultimately required for each person is a personal and definitive orientation toward God and away from evil. Is love of God and neighbor paramount or does selfishness and personal aggrandizement control and motivate so as to reject God and renounce salvation.

Ultimately, perhaps on a day when beaten down and beset by problems which seem to have no solution, they cast aside reliance on their own efforts and cry out for help from the One Who has been there always, but has largely been ignored. Then, as many another has found, He will not be silent, but will hear their plea and show them the way. For He has always been there, entreating them to turn to Him, but His voice was drowned out by the constant din of the world's alternatives.

Chapter Seven
A Note to Catholics

I would like to take a few moments to address those who were raised Catholic and have since drifted away or for one reason or another have left the Church. If, as I have argued, the Catholic Church is the true church established by the apostles, leaving the Church is no small matter. Those who have done so have taken upon themselves a serious responsibility and will need to answer for their action.

In contrast, I look at the wonderful heritage we have as Catholics, as recipients of the authentic teachings of Jesus. They were handed down from the apostles through two millennia, accompanied by God's sacraments, and safeguarded from error by the guidance of the Holy Spirit. How fortunate we are to have available to us the necessary means to achieve our salvation as we grow in love and await our eternal home in heaven.

Using a quote from an old radio program of the last century, "And now the rest of the story." The sublime vision conjured up by the above paragraph is muddled at best as we present a summary of today's reality. Many parents do insist that their children complete their initiation with the sacraments of Baptism, Penance, the

Eucharist and Confirmation. But in many cases, it is more ritual than real. Preparation to the point of valid understanding is seldom accomplished and true parental participation in mind and soul is almost totally absent. How can we conclude this? Only a small percentage of confirmed young adults seldom, if ever, darken the interior of the church once the day of Confirmation is past? What real understanding do they have of what they profess to believe and of what difference it will make whether they believe it or not?

Meanwhile the world with all its siren calls and "new knowledge and insights" blares out today's truth, not the unchanging Truth of God, and dares to have anyone contradict it. Our young are outmanned, outgunned and ridiculed, and without an oasis of calm where they can begin to see more clearly and reject the falsities of today's society. What are needed are more available sources of Truth that will lead to understanding and renewed Faith. What sources there are do not adequately address the need.

Only a small percentage of those we have lost are influenced in ways to increase their faith. Most make their infrequent appearance in church on Christmas and Easter and on special family occasions. They are often greeted with big smiles and they dutifully laugh when the priest suggests that they might come more frequently, which of course they almost never do. Now let me ask you. "Who are the foolish ones?" Jesus suffered an excruciating passion and death for our salvation. He established His Church and He left with us the means to combat the world and work out our salvation. No place did He say that if we accept Him as our Lord and Savior we are assured of salvation. On the contrary, He bid each of us to carry our cross daily and follow Him, to love Him with our whole heart and mind and strength and to demonstrate our love by obeying His commandments. He gave us the sacraments to become intimate parts of our lives.

We see evil around us at every turn. But the world sees only what it determines as evil. If we hearken back to a more believing time where God and morality were more central in our lives, where the unchanging truths of the past were not challenged and vilified, might we see that we are on a faulty path, passing through the wide gate, described in the gospel of Matthew, that leads to destruction. *Mt 7:13.*

I fear also that many who still reside within the confines of Faith, who participate and consider themselves Catholic, do so with what I might call "an absent heart". For them I recall the words from Revelation, "Would that you be either hot or cold. So because you are lukewarm, neither hot nor cold, I will spit you out of my mouth." *Rev 3:15-16.*

In today's world, where everything that we believe and hold to is challenged and vilified, to be lukewarm is to put on no armor, make no defense, and hide behind platitudes and accommodations with evil. The early Christians were made of sterner stuff. It cost to be a follower of Christ and it costs today. We are either with Christ or we are smothered into a moribund acceptance which deadens the soul and bears no fruit.

As I have said repeatedly in this book, we must seek the Truth. I state categorically that there is an issue of truth. Are those who work their way through life believing and living the Faith as it was proclaimed to many, aspiring to the eternal salvation promised to them—do they labor in vain, on a fool's errand? Or rather, are those who take the easy way, who make their own path, who believe that their knowledge and understanding exceeds that of the greatest wisdom of the past—are they the ones who walk in darkness and are in danger of stumbling into the pit?

For those of you who are on the outside, who maintain only a tenuous relationship with your Catholic Faith, you owe it to yourselves and to your children to seek that Truth that will set you free. Vast amounts of information are readily available and the depth of the understanding that can be obtained is great. What is required is the will to seek and you will find, and the humility to ask and you will be heard. If you are drunk with the pleasures and allurements of this world then these words may well fall on deaf ears. But in a moment when the Divine Light comes upon you, would that you will answer and find your true home.

PART TWO

Introduction

In Part One I provided a rationale for assessing the options for preparing for eternity. I reviewed the claims of atheists and rebuttals for their assertions. I presented a discussion on the nature of God and immutability of Truth. I presented evidence of God's revelation to man through the history of His chosen people, the Jewish Nation, and through the history of the man who claimed to be God's Son, Jesus Christ. I explored the history of the Church he established, the Catholic Church, and the fracturing of that Church through the Eastern Orthodox Schism and the Protestant Reformation. I also reviewed the current state of belief among Catholics. I repeatedly urged the readers to sincerely and prayerfully investigate to find their truth and to chart their life's course based on their results.

If after considering the material presented in Part One, the reader still has decided to adhere to an atheistic course, I urge him to keep an open mind and to continue to humbly seek the Truth. God is patient and will not abandon him but will always provide a way if he would only seek to find it. For those who want to follow Jesus, the way is spelled out in the New Testament. But we must seek the truth revealed in the written word with the aid of those who can interpret that word. As I have stated in Part One, unguided interpretations lead to errors promulgated by false teachers, teachers who often deny Tradition, the oral interpretation of the Word passed down from the apostles and those who knew and learned from them. In addition, there will always be those who preach a new way, not in keeping with that taught by the apostles, but according to that espoused by these false teachers. What credibility do they have, those who claim such new truths in contradiction to the Word taught by Jesus?

We are told in the gospel preached by Jesus and the apostles that faith is a gift from God and that not all are given that gift. Those who are given the gift of faith are like those in the gospel parable who are given gold talents and are expected to invest those talents and provide to their master fruit of their labors. The one who does nothing with his gift and buries it in the ground is condemned for his laziness and lack of effort. If we have been given faith we are expected to evangelize and preach the word we have been given, and more importantly live in accordance with that word.

But not all are given faith. Are they then exempt from any responsibility? The gospel does not say that. We will be judged based on what we have been given and how we have responded to that gift. If we sit idle or make no effort to find the Truth and live accordingly, we will be like the unprofitable servant of the parable and will be condemned. Some may make excuses like, "Didn't we cast out demons in your name," to which Jesus responded, "I do not know you." *Mt 7:22-23*. He responded that way because their works were evil. They claimed to love Jesus but did not keep his word. As St. James said in the Letter of James, "Faith without works is dead." *Jas 2:26*.

In Part Two, we will consider how to live as the children of God and to attain an everlasting crown. If we have chosen the path to a loving God Who greatly desires our salvation, what course will we take to ensure that we are granted that salvation. We do not want to be like those in the parable of the sower who went out to plant his seed and let some seed fall on the roadside. The birds came and took away the seed. Jesus likened this situation to those who hear the Word of God and let the devil take the word from them; or like the seed which fell on rocky ground which had no root and died, which he likened to those who heard the word but had no conviction and abandoned the word in time of strife or difficulty. Nor will we want to be like the seed which fell among thorns and was choked out, which Jesus likened to those who lost their faith because of their attachment to riches and other things of this world. We want to be like those who, like the seed which fell on fertile ground, hear the Word, rejoice and yield 30, 60 or 100-fold.

It is not that we might plan or want to abandon our belief in and love of Jesus, but actions we take during our lives can make us vulnerable to bad consequences and weaken our resolve to follow Jesus. In the following chapters we will discuss a number of areas which are critically important in charting our course toward salvation and avoiding those obstacles and actions which could thwart our efforts. To live a fruitful life, we must live a disciplined life in which we have a firm control of our passions and desires. It is a life in which we sincerely love our neighbor, and in which we give to God the worship and honor and obedience He deserves and requires if we are to be called children of God and heirs to eternal happiness with Him for all eternity.

In our current age there are many who have charted their own course and written their own moral code. They flaunt the exhortations from Paul in his Epistle to the Galatians, who enumerates the works of the flesh as "fornication, impurity, licentiousness, idolatry, sorcery, enmity, strife, jealousy, anger, selfishness, dissensions, factions, envy, drunkenness, carousing and the like. I warn you...that those who do such things shall not inherit the kingdom of God." *Gal 5:19-21*. They are the false teachers condemned by Peter in his Second Epistle, "who will introduce destructive heresies and even deny the Master Who ransomed them, bringing swift destruction on themselves. Many will follow their licentious ways and because of them the way of truth will be reviled." 2 Pt 2:1-2. They deceive those who are vulnerable and cause them to believe untruths which can lead them to great unhappiness and imperil their eternal salvation.

Chapter One
The Presence of Evil

Before I begin a discussion of the attributes of a well-lived life it is important to fully come to grips with the problem of evil. To quote from St. Paul's Epistle to the Romans: "I see in my members another principle at war with the law of my mind taking me captive to the law of sin that dwells in my members." *Rm 7:23*. It is this principle which subjects each of us to inclinations to commit harmful acts on ourselves and on others. How well we control these inclinations is a critical factor in determining our happiness in this life and our ultimate path to eternity.

The first step in controlling these inclinations is to admit their presence and accept our responsibility to control them. Many, however, do not see them as obstacles to a good life but rather embrace them as desired elements to be used in the pursuit of pleasure, riches, power and a host of other goals. The more these pursuits continue unabated the more each person becomes a slave to them and their ability to free themselves becomes more and more difficult. The end result, which we witness over and over in the public square, is a tragic replay of the same scenario. Celebrities with great talent and potential lose themselves in dissolute living, always looking for something never acquired, but always coming up short. Descending irrevocably to lower and lower depths of depravity and unhappiness they end their lives a stark antithesis to what could have been.

Sometimes the story has a happier ending if the person gets needed help from others or undergoes a basic change in outlook caused by a spiritual awakening. It is this spiritual awakening which is so important to give the resolve to living a disciplined life and to provide the insight and belief to proceed along such a way before entering a destructive path like that described above.

A more common occurrence is one of indifference. The person does not see himself as evil but has no desire to necessarily improve his way of life to be better than he currently is. He cherishes his freedom to do pretty much as he likes and gives little heed to the consequences. This approach rings well with modern audiences who cherish their freedoms and independence but has serious shortcomings when dealing with life and death issues of who we are and where we are going. It minimizes the importance of God in the picture. Does He not have a final say in what is good or bad? Does He not determine ultimately the end result of our existence?

If we have come to accept that there is a God Who has deigned to give us life and the promise of an eternity with Him in bliss and glory, has He not established the provisions necessary to achieve that eternal life? How is it that many have taken it upon themselves to define what they can and cannot do to obtain eternal life? What authority do they have for doing so?

Part of the answer lies in a current state of denial by many that there is no sin but that perhaps defined by a general consensus of society. Some have "evolved" in their understanding and thus now state that what was sin before is no longer so. That fact that this action flies in the face of the eternal and unchanging nature of Truth does not deter them in any way. They continue on unabated with an arrogance and righteousness which would outdo the biblical Pharisees.

A second and extremely important element in any discussion of evil is the devil. Here again, many will deny or lampoon the existence of evil spirits or in contrast, will engage in activities directly engaging with such spirits. Anyone who has taken the time to investigate the existence of such beings and see the great harm they can cause, will know that they do exist and that to engage with them in any way will lead to great spiritual harm. Books on exorcisms—the casting out of evil spirits from those possessed—and the experience of exorcists have shown decisively the power of these beings and the great hatred they have for God and all that is good. Fr. Gabriele Amorth, for many years the chief exorcist in the City of Rome, Italy, has written a book entitled, *An Exorcist Tells His Story,* in which he describes his many experiences and provides a detailed introduction into what we believe as Christians about the devil and his angels.

The examples Fr. Amorth relates are chilling, to say the least. Experiences of those who have been possessed by evil spirits include the ability to speak unknown languages exhibit great strength or have knowledge unknown to others. Their condition is tragic. They are no longer in control of their bodies and they are frequently deemed to be suffering from mental illness, rather than possession. Only those trained in recognizing the differences in the two conditions can effectively help the affected individuals. Those consorting with sorcerers, witches and others dealing in the occult put themselves in danger of great harm. Fr. Amorth emphasizes that there is no "white magic" that is totally good or harmless. All occult activity is due to evil spirits who hate God and seek only harm to those who would deal with them.

For those wanting to explore further the works of the devil Fr. Amorth has written a second book entitled, *An Exorcist, More Stories.* Both books provide important information that can put into a clearer perspective the evil present in our world and ways to avoid its results.

We cannot answer the question as to why God allows these spirits to be with us. We believe in accordance with the Scripture that they will be consigned to hell at the end of time, but until that time they will be with us, as Peter describes in his Second Epistle, "The devil goes around like a roaring lion seeking whom he can devour." *2 Pt 5:8*

The following chapter on suffering continues the preparatory discussions of Part Two. We will see that suffering is a direct result of evil acts caused by some. They have free will and often exercise that free will to the harm of others. The devil also incessantly works to cause us harm and to thwart God's plan, often causing great suffering. Many cry, "Why O Lord do you allow this?" We cannot answer except to bow to the wisdom of God who created all with a divine purpose and plan which is beyond our comprehension.

Chapter Two
Suffering

One of the most contentious areas of discussion in the world today is why there is so much suffering. Many have tried to address the presence of suffering from a variety of perspectives. Some postulate that a loving God would not have allowed suffering and thus they conclude that there is no God. They trumpet this conclusion even though their first premise is pulled out of thin air with not a thread of truth to support it. Thus, their logic is seriously flawed. In many Protestant congregations the belief exists that if one experiences suffering then the cause is that they are lacking in faith and that with a more perfect faith they would reduce or eliminate their suffering.

As was discussed in the previous chapter much suffering results from the free will that God has given to His creatures. They are directed by God to love one another, but they can refuse. They are directed to reject evil, but they can embrace it and in doing so can bring great harm on themselves and on others. As was also discussed, the devil is always working to thwart God's plan and is responsible for instigating evil actions on the part of many, causing great suffering.

On a more personal level an individual response can be combative, angry or accepting, depending largely on one's religious beliefs. But though many conflicting answers are put forth to explain the presence of suffering we are largely unable to give a satisfactory answer. In the minds of many God should not have allowed all of this suffering. Why couldn't everyone be made such that they would respond positively to God's Word? But that would have curtailed free will and was not in accordance with God's plan.

In the Book of Job in the Old Testament we read of a just man. Job, whom God allows the devil to beset with many misfortunes, including the loss of his children, his property and his bodily health. He is further counseled by his friends that he must have done something wrong to have deserved his punishment. He denies this but later, in response to the repeated urgings of his friends, Job brings his complaint directly to God.

God's response is direct and unequivocal. God asks him where he was when the foundations of the world were laid, when the myriad of events occurred during the eons of time during which the world was created and formed into its present state. It soon becomes clear to Job that he stands unable to answer and becomes mute and accepting of God's omniscience and wisdom.

In the epilogue we see that Job is returned to double his previous wealth and receives more abundant blessings in his later years than he had before.

In David Limbaugh's book, *The Emmaus Code*, referenced earlier, the author addresses the question as to why God chose to enable our salvation through our own cooperation, rather than by ensuring it through no effort on our own. He emphasizes that Scripture clearly indicates that God refines us through our experiences and references Isaiah, "Behold, I have refined you, but not as silver, I have tried you in the furnace of affliction". *Isa 48:10.* In His supreme wisdom God chose this path as the better way.

I would like to propose a perspective that I hope some will find helpful. We begin with a well-known passage from Paul's Epistle to the Philippians: *Phil 2:6-9*

> *Christ, though He was in the form of God, did not regard His equality with God something to be grasped—he humbled himself becoming obedient to death, even death on a cross.*
>
> *Because of this God greatly exalted Him and bestowed on him a name which is above every name.*

Christ endured intense pain leading to an ignoble death in perfect acceptance of the will of His Father. In the garden of Gethsemane Jesus asked, "My Father, if it is not possible that this cup pass from me without my drinking it, your will be done." Mt 26:42. As a result, he has been glorified by the Father. Christ bids us to take up our cross daily and follow him. Christ has told us that the servant is not greater than the master and that we can expect suffering to befall us. But we can also look forward to glory resulting from our obedience to the will of the Father. What is most important is to accept, as did Job, God's Divine Wisdom which knows all and determines all and will eventually bring us to eternal life.

Chapter Three
A Disciplined Life

In the Book of Proverbs in the Old Testament we see it stated that the beginning of wisdom is "the fear of the Lord." *Prv 9:10.* Let us reflect on that statement for a few moments. The Lord God is the source of all truth and goodness and all creatures are subject to His authority. In justice all must abide by His decrees and their actions will receive their rightful recompense. A clear realization that our actions have consequences can be extremely beneficial in helping us to control our innate tendencies toward selfishness and disregard for the good of others.

In the case of the child, the parent is the usual authority figure and direction given lovingly but firmly can begin a process to control the actions of the child and instill in him a sense of well-being resulting from a habitual adherence to accepted norms of conduct and the concomitant responsibility to participate as a fully integrated member in society. It is the breakdown or lack of a positive authority figure which can result in lack of discipline and a rejection of authority, leading to serious future problems.

We have all seen cases where parents have been unwilling to discipline their children, giving in to their incessant demands for more and more things and greater and greater freedom to do as they like. Sometimes the parents are so engrossed in their own lives that they delegate their responsibilities to others, assuming that if they provide all of the material needs that their duties have been fulfilled. In doing so they frequently let the child pick up whatever guidance they can from their caregivers, but denying them a clear understanding of why?

I want to take a few paragraphs to emphasize this last point. A child will frequently ask why they need to do a particular task or act in a particular way. If the answer given is frivolous or unintelligible the child remains unconvinced that it is required and will object or seek to avoid compliance at every opportunity. Once, a friend of mine, a father, told his child in answer to the question, "It's because I'm bigger than you." We all laughed when we heard it, but should have realized that the child deserved a better answer.

Clarity of vision is key for anyone to accept an answer given to their honest question. Depending on the age of the questioner a detailed answer may not be given at the time but an adequate answer should be given commensurate with the age or understanding of the individual. Let's say a child has hit another child. We can reprove the child by explaining that if he acts that way he can expect to be hit back and that he or the other child could be injured. Great unhappiness on his part or on the part of his parents could result and he wouldn't want that.

We could say that we are all called and expected to love each other and that not hitting another child is a requirement if we want to live as God commands us to live.

For some children that above approach could be quite effective and if built upon could lead to a well-adjusted individual. Some children will be much more obstinate and a more deliberative effort could well be required, including disciplinary steps to get the child's attention while continuing to deal with the child with love and reasoned discussion. Years ago, I heard of one couple who had two children who behaved beautifully and they were the envy of other parents who were having much more difficulty in managing their children. Then the couple had a third child and everything changed. The child was head-strong and opposed them at every turn and they no longer blissfully assumed that they were the gifted ones when it came to raising children.

Notice that I introduced a moral standard in the above discussion. For many, adherence to a God-centered standard can provide a foundation and justification for required norms of conduct. Absent some standard what is to prevent the child from resorting to selfish motives when presented with choices of action? In today's society the need for a firm foundation is absolutely necessary. There will be calls on all sides to engage in activities which are immoral and self-injurious. We see the multiple and tragic drug and opioid deaths that are experienced every year.

What I don't hear is the answer to the question, "Why do they take these drugs which can kill them?"

The effort to establish discipline in one's life is a long-term process and can continue for a lifetime. Self-denial is the way we can hone our will to withstand the onslaught of our passions and our desire for self-gratification. If we never deny ourselves anything then we have little or no will power. When we are tempted to do something we would rather not do, we have no resistance and yield to the temptation. Those who come from wealth or those who through their fame or stardom become the darlings of society, can seem impervious for a time to serious consequences for their actions. But eventually they too can commit a serious offense and must bear the consequences.

More importantly, the lack of discipline destroys the fabric of one's moral base and seriously damages their relation with God. God's mercy will always be there but if the damage is too great will the person realize that the welfare of their soul is in the balance and will they act before the Lord calls them home?

The tragic results stemming from undisciplined behavior are in the news daily. The questions are always asked. Why did this happen? Who is responsible? What should have been done? Usually the problem has been present in childhood and was quite apparent to those who had seen similar characteristics in other children, with similar end results. But those in authority either did not see or did not believe that there was a problem. But more importantly, there was likely no moral compass, no generally accepted and societal norm which would have worked to modify the direction being taken by the child.

What is perplexing is how often such persons are found to be attractive to others and become involved in relationships which are injurious to the happiness of both parties. The signs are evident to those who care to look that relationships with potential partners who are short tempered, controlling, inconsiderate or unsociable are very likely to be difficult, if not impossible, to be harmonious and will result in turmoil and even violence.

Without discipline no task can be done well and a concerted effort is required to achieve any successful result. Anyone involved with sports or the arts knows that without prolonged and intensive efforts no achievement of any consequence will result. But with commitment and perseverance good progress can be made. Perhaps surprisingly, once the mind and body become more and more disciplined the effort becomes more routine and accepted. The benefit seen as a result of the applied effort provides a satisfaction and sense of well–being that provides additional encouragement, and the process can continue to redound to the benefit of the person.

The difficulty is getting the cooperation and commitment of the undisciplined person to begin the process. If they have grown to adulthood with serious character flaws and few moral qualms they have little interest in changing and without a serious circumstance which forces them to act they persist in their current state. It may be a health crisis or the death of a loved one or a spiritual awakening where the person finally realizes that they are in serious trouble and that without Divine help they will flounder and experience serious harm.

The positive fruit of discipline is responsibility. A disciplined person who is no longer a slave to his emotions and desires becomes free to consider his relationship with others and his position in the world around him. He begins to see that his actions can have beneficial outcomes and at times will become necessary to fulfill his obligations to others. The greater this realization the more the person attains his place as a fully contributing member of our human society.

Chapter Four
The Tyranny of the Passions

One of the most important choices a person can make is whether or not they will be mastered by their passions. During childhood, if we are fortunate, we learn self-control and come to see the importance of controlling those instincts which can lead us into serious trouble. For reasons we cannot fully explain children do not come equal with regard to their innate tendencies. One child is quiet and introspective. Another is outspoken and strong willed. Parental success in regard to one child may be greatly diminished in the case of another, even though similar methods of rearing may be employed. The shortcomings of the parents also result in strong influences which can largely override even basically good parenting.

One parent may be an alcoholic. Another may be extremely controlling. A third may overly favor one child over another for reasons which are never explained or admitted to. Whatever the cause, many children reach teenage or early adulthood with flaws in their character which can lead to unfortunate consequences.

The point of this essay is not to delve into a lengthy discussion on the causes of the above character flaws but rather to make the case to young adults who are faced with making life changing choices, that despite their current condition they have the power to change and become productive and happy adults. But they must choose wisely and have available to them good sources of information given by others who ascribe to them the dignity they deserve, and who love them and want to help them. They must further realize that there will be many who will want to lead them in ways which may appear to offer some fleeting relief from the pain and anguish they may be suffering but which in reality will lead them inevitably into greater unhappiness.

The most prevalent obstacles to one's achieving a full and upright life are addictions to alcohol and other opiates, uncontrolled and/or indiscriminate sex, mental illness, depression and the unhappiness resulting from the lack of love in their life. Help from others will frequently be needed by those afflicted, enabling them to see more clearly the state they are in and indicating to them ways that they can begin to find a way back to a meaningful and fulfilling existence.

For many, there is a conviction that they are of little or no worth. Perhaps they were never given reasons to love themselves or appreciate the talents they have and now consider themselves unable to be loved by others. God may be unknown to them either because of some atheistic belief which they have acquired or because they think that God has abandoned them or would no longer forgive them because of their actions. Many suicides are believed to have been caused by those thinking they are of no worth and, in despair, have chosen to end their lives. We have vivid testimonies of those who have survived suicide attempts or who have been dissuaded from doing so by others at the last minute.

Only through love can they become rehabilitated. The love shown to them by others can begin to change their perspective but it can be a long process. They must first take full responsibility for what they may have done and to then begin to believe that they are worthy of redemption. Belief in a loving God can be invaluable to them and will give them a strong incentive to conquer their addiction and grow in love and acceptance of who they are and why their life is worth living.

For those who are enslaved to their addiction, it is only when the realization comes that they are on a tragic path that perhaps some will seek an alternative. It is to those that I appeal to take the first step. You have nothing to lose and your eventual happiness is well worth the effort. Look for help from those you have come to trust, from those who love you for who you are, not for what you can do for them. If you have faith in God, pray for help and have confidence that you will obtain that help. Many before you have succeeded and you can too. As Jesus said, "Not one sparrow falls from the sky without God knowing it, and you are worth more than many sparrows". *Mt 10:29.*

Chapter Five
The Ways of Love

Love is one of the most overworked words in the English language. It can be used to mean a strong liking, a sexual attraction, an altruistic commitment or a sincere desire for the good of another person. It is this last definition that we will dwell on in this current discussion. To paraphrase the words of St. Paul, in his First Epistle to the Corinthians, love is patient, kind, not inflated or rude, does not seek its own interests, does not brood over injury, does not rejoice over wrong doing but rejoices in the Truth.

All of the meanings mentioned, except the last, are influenced to varying degrees by the desires or feelings of the lover. Thus the "love" expressed can quickly change if the desired recipient rejects it, and its opposite, hate can easily result. But when centered in the good of another the purpose of love does not change with the response of the intended recipient. The good of the other person is still a desirable result and still has intrinsic value even though one giving the love finds it much more difficult to continue to do so.

Jesus commands us to love one another. Early Christians demonstrated this love to such an extent that the pagans would remark in amazement, "See how they love one another." Loving others we come in contact with is made much easier if we have humility. The more realistically we assess ourselves with our shortcomings as well as our talents the more we can appreciate the good that is present in others. Some seem to think that they are God's special gift to humanity and that all should tell them this at all times. Do they not realize that they have nothing which they did not receive? Rather than basking in the glow of their talents, should they not work even harder. We should always remember that if we have gifts we are expected to use them for the benefit of others and show the Lord Who gave us the gifts that we have been worthy servants.

Let us expand on this line of thought when we relate it to relationships between men and women. It is quite natural that men and women are initially attracted to each other because of appearances, demeanor, talents or any of a number of different elements. There may be a rush of emotion, a desire for a closer relationship and an exhilaration that a potential partner or confidant may have been found. We may even call it "love at first sight." But it is not the love referred to by Paul. This does not mean it is bad, but it is very dependent on the beneficial effect perceived or expected by the lover. To some extent, then, it is tentative and easily subject to change as more becomes known about the intended object of the affection.

Assume then that the relationship quickly becomes sexual in nature, which is all too common in today's world. As long as the sexual attraction continues and there are no strong alternative influences that work against the relationship the two lovers will be happy. But as time goes on the relationship must develop other common goals which augment the sexual relationship. Perhaps there are similar work or creative interests, common friends and activities, and if the relationship lasts long enough, children. But are these ties of a type and a constancy which will endure through periods of misfortune, illness, or moral weakness?

What, one may ask, is the one fundamental tie which will be more important than all others? The answer is *commitment.* For this reason was the marriage vow an integral part of any permanent relationship between a man and a women. Commitment, if truly held and believed in, will provide bedrock in time of adversity. It will withstand the headwinds of misfortune, selfishness, sickness and human shortcomings. But the commitment must be sincere and entered into with adequate knowledge and reflection. It cannot be just enunciated dutifully as part of a ceremony, then quickly forgotten and never more brought to mind.

Some may ask if the love described by St. Paul can actually be achieved within the married state. It may sound fine if we apply this paradigm to the priestly or religious communities but can it apply to the more common married state? The answer is a resounding YES. But it will not happen all at once or without effort. But it will be worth it!

So what is the secret? Actually, there is no secret. How does one achieve anything of value? Inspiration, knowledge, hard work and commitment to the final objective—these are the watchwords. And what should be the final objective? If one wants a spouse, a soul mate, a confidant, a lover for life—the final objective is a union of mind and heart in a relationship devoted to the welfare and happiness of the couple. It cannot be a his or hers, a mine or yours, a my good vs. your good. As the Scripture says, "It shall be two in one flesh". *Gen 2:24.*

If one wants to find a partner for life they should have a good idea of what they are looking for and the model they have in mind is critical. If they emphasize attractiveness rather than wholesomeness, if they are looking for a good time rather than family time, if they believe that the size of the house they want is more important than the ones who will live in it, than that is likely what they will get. But they shouldn't expect to have a family modeled after the biblical exhortation, "two in one flesh." That relationship requires an altering of priorities.

If one puts their own good above that of their intended partner, they will not succeed. To grow in love, one must make himself vulnerable and be willing to sacrifice for the good of the other. The only thing which should be more important than your relationship with your partner is your relationship with God. Would that your God would hold a place in your lives as does my God because there is no contradiction in putting God first since no one can be more loving and more supportive of your relationship than God.

What a great gift it is to grow old together with one's spouse. In a world where the young and youth are idolized and old age frequently brings sickness and loneliness the blessing of a loving and truly supportive spouse cannot be overemphasized. When the distractions of youthful desires, ambitions, welfare of children and personal goals subside what are we left with as we await eternity? With a loving spouse we have a foretaste of the next life, a hint of what is in store for those who love God—where we will be loved without conditions, without measure and without end.

Chapter Six
Marriage Today

With more and more couples living together without the benefit of a marriage certificate what was once an important choice in the lives of many young people has been delayed indefinitely—whether or not they will get married. Though in the short term, couples are happily, or perhaps unhappily, exchanging partners, whatever long-term effects that may result are not being addressed or even considered. Certainly, the underlying concept of marriage has been jettisoned to the trash heap and replaced by empirical "let's try living together and if we seem to fit well we can decide then whether or not we want to make things permanent."

The biblical concept of "two in one flesh", indicating an intimate relationship of heart, mind and affection has been replaced by what appears to be a compatibility quotient of sorts related to sex, temperament and space. We have a satisfactory sexual relationship. We don't fight, at least not often. And we both have space to be who we are.

I think this last point is the key factor. If I choose to live with someone who may up and leave at any time I certainly want to provide some protection to myself if things don't work out, so that the other person does not divulge personal information that could be injurious to me. But the fact that I need space for the personal me will always result in a persistent barrier preventing the very intimacy that I inwardly want but am afraid to actively seek.

Some will no doubt counter that they have achieved intimacy and at some point, have decided that they wanted and eventually moved to a permanent relationship in marriage. But many more have not, and have transitioned from one partner to another, never fully committing to a permanent bond. Another troubling result is that many times one partner will not under any circumstances make a permanent commitment. The other keeps hoping, even to the point of having children, that they can coax their reluctant mate to propose, only to eventually see that they will be disappointed.

The high divorce rate among those who marry has been pointed to as the reason why many young men and women do not want the expense and heartbreak of the marriage/divorce syndrome and opt for informal relationships. They can seemingly get the fruit of companionship and limited intimacy with little investment other than a temporary agreement worked out with the intended partner.

The cultural upheaval over the last half century has indeed torn away at the underlying fabric of the marriage relationship. Rather than building on the bedrock of unselfish love and undying commitment as in times past, we have substituted relationships of convenience. We have cast children into a maze of parents and step-parents, step-brothers and step-sisters, new families and separated families, single parents and substitute (grand) parents. The list goes on and on. We likely have as many divorces as before. The brave new world is listing badly and few seem to notice.

The past did not have all joy and goodness. But if some came up short it was because they did not abide by the well-known and accepted moral underpinnings of society. Families flourished, even in hard times, because there was a wholesomeness and shared responsibility to work for the common good of the family unit. Older members could look forward to spending declining years in the company of devoted spouses.

Again, we go back to the words from the Bible, "two in one flesh." These do not present just a poetic fantasy. As human beings we need to belong, to love others, especially the one we have chosen as a spouse. It is in loving that we become more fully alive to why we were created and why we are here. Marriage is the avenue where most will find their ultimate destiny, if they will search for it, yearn for it and subjugate their devotion to self to the welfare of another.

If we contemplate for a few moments on the coming years, what of those who have never married, but drifted through life with an array of relationships, none permanent, and find themselves alone with only casual relationships. Perhaps they will see that a life of receiving and giving little, a life of ambiguity rather than commitment, an overarching love of self rather than of others, has a bitter aftertaste. It could have been so much better but was squandered at the altar of self.

Chapter Seven
The Blessing of Children

What a great privilege and blessing it is to join with God in the creation of another human being formed from a union of love within the marriage bond. So it has been through past millennia until our modern era, when in our sophistication we have charted a new course.

Children are now, by many, believed to be unwanted burdens, restrictions on our freedoms, and the source of unneeded, undesired responsibilities. The Divine command to "increase and multiply" has been subjugated to the mantra of raising children that are wanted and do not overly affect our desired lifestyles and goals.

In times past children were a greatly desired gift from God, who could advance the welfare of a family, extend the lineage and provide parental support in old age. They often grew up in difficult circumstances and learned first-hand the need for discipline, responsibility and a strong moral compass to allow them to function and prosper in the world.

Today the emphasis is often on cost—how much money required to clothe, feed, house and educate a child—frequently publicized in the press. Societal pressures weight heavily on the parents to provide the many technological and material resources so that the child can participate in the many wonderful benefits of living in our modern world. But the result has been a fracturing of the family unit. Life has progressed to being an incessant marathon of required milestones, all indicative of the child's advancement along a designated path—to participate in many activities, to get a good education, to get into a good college, to get a good job, to marry and to raise a family with enough money available so that they can have the best of everything. These are not bad things in themselves, but the emphasis on material things leaves little time for advancement in spiritual things.

We are in serious jeopardy of losing the sense of awe in the act that we have been a part of. We have become pragmatic, looking at the growing child through a lens colored by our own dreams and desires. We say we want only the best for our child—but who's best? Is it our goal that the child be filled with love of God and love of the great gift of life he has been given?

As we grow old what do we expect from our children? If we have been so busy working and providing them with the best of material things but have not given them of ourselves, do they really know who we are and what we believe? If we caused ourselves to be mired totally in material pursuits then our children will be there also. But how does such a state relate to our ultimate goals as we approach eternity. Will we be judged on how much money our children were able earn, how much prestige they acquired in the world, or rather on what kind of persons they grew up to be? Will they be filled with love and have a vibrant and close relationship with their God or will they be a stranger to Him.

In today's world rearing a child is much more difficult than many realize. Not too many years ago it was a familiar axiom that it took a village to raise a child. The belief was that the goodness, the integrity and commonly-held principles sustaining the inhabitants of the village would nurture the teachings of the parents and provide a reinforcement of the child's formation. Today the watchwords must be vigilance and persistence to nullify corrosive and disruptive influences from a society with few restraints on conduct and advocating alternatives to what the parents are trying to teach. Even under the best of circumstances the ever-present toxic influences are difficult to combat and if the parental efforts are minimal or non-existent the predictable results are often tragic.

What are required today are parents who are grounded in faith and having an over-riding love of God and their neighbor, and who want most for their child true happiness of mind and soul in this life and eternal happiness with God forever. With great disappointment we see that in many cases that is not the case and we also hear the increasing lament that what could have been will never be.

If the child is to be filled with love then we must show the way. Our life must illuminate the way, a way of growth in love and an emerging realization that without love all else pales in value. How do we grow in love? We grow by loving others. The child needs our love. The child thrives on our love, is dependent on our love. The more we love the child the more our love is reciprocated and the more we grow in love. But let us not equate love with things. If we give things, but not ourselves; if we want to live vicariously through the child, that is not love. Love is for the benefit of the recipient of that love and thinks only of the recipient.

What a wonderful gift to be able to form an everlasting bond of love with another human being that we have helped create. What a tragedy to have had such an opportunity and to have squandered it in the pursuit of pleasure and selfish desires. The one thing that lasts is love—not fame, not accomplishment. A child formed in the loving embrace of God will shine through all eternity as the fruit of a loving union and as a testimony to the love which he has received.

Chapter Eight
Impediments to Spiritual Growth

Refusal to Forgive

Do you hold a grudge against anyone? Is there a relative or friend that you don't speak to anymore because of something they did to you?

Every time we recite the Lord's Prayer we state that we forgive those who trespass against us (Catholic version) just as we ask God to forgive our offenses. But if we are holding back from forgiving someone, we are speaking a falsehood.

Refusal to forgive can have many reasons. We may have been hurt, disappointed, embarrassed, falsely accused. Perhaps we have been defrauded, denied something due to us. So how does Christ's command to love one another affect our response?

If I love someone, I want good to result for that person. If I forgive them the wrong they have done to me, it can have a positive effect. Rather than returning anger for anger they are left feeling small and totally in the wrong. This does not mean that there is not an issue of justice here that I will address in the next section.

What then is the cost to me if I forgive? I deny myself whatever satisfaction I might gain from remaining unforgiving and angry. This is certainly hard but not injurious to me, except to my pride. And how hopeful I can be as I stand before God and ask His forgiveness for my offences!

Justice

There is a question of justice. In St. Paul's Epistle to the Romans we read, "Vengeance is mine, says the Lord." *Rm 12:19*. God will requite all for their actions. We can be sure of that. But many do not want to abide by God's promise. They want their own satisfaction and want to administer their own justice. How often have we seen those harmed in the public square condemn the evildoers in no uncertain terms, often to the depth of hell with no chance of redemption. As we see from St. Paul's epistle, we are not given that authority. In cases of material harm done to a person, there is rightly justice to be administered by the state, acting in proper authority.

Reconciliation

"Blessed are the peacemakers, for they shall be called 'children of God'". The quote from Christ's Sermon on the Mount, *Mt 5:9,* points out to us the special place given to those who would work toward reconciliation between quarreling parties. Where there have been wrongs committed, how fruitful can be a cessation of animosity and bitterness. One side must make the first move. There may be rejection, even hostility, but the great benefit is worth the effort. Only those who have made that first overture can truly attest to the lasting blessing that can result.

Lack of Repentance

"Have mercy on me God in your goodness. In your abundant compassion blot out my offense." *Ps 51:3.* Those who approach the Lord in accordance with the words of the psalm can have confidence that He will hear them and forgive their offences. But what if they don't believe they have offended; or what if they believe He will forgive them simply because they are His people and thus He will overlook their offences? But how could they believe that they have not offended Him? They have disobeyed His commandments and they have frequently flouted His laws. How could they not have heard His words, "Repent, or you will perish"? *Lk 13:7.*

We live in a world of disbelief. Many go their own way and do what they want. Their vision is clouded and their will is obstinate. Yet, they say they believe and that they are God's people. They want to belong and be counted with the elect, but on their own terms. I say that because many want to alter the laws that they have been taught. As stated earlier, some have "evolved" in their understanding and have changed their interpretation of what is required. Others see no need for previous guidelines and practices. They believe that there is no need to work to be perfect in accordance with the words of Jesus, "Be ye perfect as your heavenly Father is perfect". *Mt 5:48.* But we are commanded to demonstrate our love of Jesus by keeping His commandments. In doing so, we strive each day to become more perfect and ultimately achieve the goal for which we were created—to achieve salvation.

For those of you who are parents, don't the responses above sound like the words of your children? We can expect those responses from children but not from those who call themselves the people of God. The evil that abounds today will not be thwarted by making shortcuts around the words of the gospel. Did we not see over and over the results when the children of Israel tried to go their own way and corrupted themselves?

To be truly repentant we must stop making excuses and neglecting our duties to God and to our fellow human beings. If we are selfish, we must become generous. If we are unbelieving, we must seek truth. We must pray as we have never prayed before. As Father Peyton in the last century said over and over, "More things are wrought by prayer than this world dreams of."

The hour is late. Sin abounds and pain and suffering are all around us. We can curse the darkness and apostatize. We can look for specious answers from those who have already led us astray. Or we can go back to the font of all goodness and joy and peace. Seek the Lord where He may be found. Follow in His footsteps and proclaim to all in a rising chorus, "Jesus is Lord!"

Presumption

When I use the word presumption I refer to the very common attempt people make to conjure up in their own minds Who God is, what He is like and as a result, what He will do in different situations. A few movies over the years have depicted God as a quaint elderly gentleman who seems quite nice, susceptible to human protestations and not one Who would likely condemn someone to eternal loss. The fact is that such a portrait of God is the result of human fantasy more than reality.

This is *not* to state that God is not merciful. He loves us more than we know and He has established from all eternity His plan for creation based on Love. It is a love of high perfection and has as its objective the good of all of God's people. As a result, it must always be tempered with justice. How can one do evil to another and as a result not incur some retribution? In the Sistine Chapel, at the Vatican, in the center of Michelangelo's ceiling we see the spark of life passing from a loving God the Father to Adam. But we also see in Michelangelo's Last Judgment, behind the altar, a stern and victorious Jesus who will judge all at the end of time.

In the Book of Psalms in the Old Testament, God responds to the Israelites who did not agree with His decrees. "As high as the heavens are above the earth so also are my ways above your ways." *Ps 103:11*. What a folly it is for human beings to impugn God's authority, to stand in opposition to His ways, and with unfathomable arrogance attempt to countermand His decrees.

It is instructive to reflect on these words from the Book of Sirach in the Old Testament:

Say not, "I have sinned, but what has befallen me?" for the Lord bides His time. Of forgiveness, be not overconfident adding sin upon sin. Say not, "Great is His mercy, my many sins He will forgive. For mercy and anger alike are with Him, upon the wicked alights His wrath. Sir 5:4-7

How do we determine the morality of our actions? Do we look for authoritative sources? Do we agonize over the rightness of our decisions? Or do we "do it my way—I know God will understand".

Referring again to the Book of Proverbs in the Old Testament we see again that the basis of wisdom is "the fear of the Lord." This statement speaks volumes. From the depth of God's perfection flows forth His omniscient will to bring all things into the perfection for which they were created. Each of us has a purpose and a place in God's eternity. We can take our place as living members of the new world that will replace our present existence, but only if we heed the will of the Father. He will not force us. But as the supreme Authority He will give to each his reward, based on his actions. Fear the Lord Who will hear the cries of those who call for justice. Fear the Lord Who sees into the inmost reaches of our soul. Fear the Lord Who will assign a place for us if we truly love Him and keep His Word.

Pride

We live in a highly competitive world and many extol themselves in being able to outdo the efforts of others. It is often tempting for them to attribute most, if not all, of their success to their own efforts with little regard to the source and purpose of what they have been given. They are like the servant in Jesus' parable who received the five talents but instead of earning another five for their master, they claim the entire benefit for themselves. Their success breeds in them a sense of superiority over others and as a result causes them to resist loving and having concern for others they come in contact with.

To truly become a child of God requires humility, the exact opposite of what drives and consumes the proud person. With humility we can relate to others and grow in love as we are commanded to do. We can see clearly that on our own we are nothing, but with God's help we can accomplish great things for His honor and glory and for the benefit of others. Thus, we can avoid becoming so consumed with our own greatness that we reject God's graces, and demand going along a different path.

Satan was the greatest of the angels and would not serve God as he was commanded to do. According to the Book of Revelation in the Bible he was cast from heaven to earth with all of the angels who followed him. *Rev 12:7-9.* The proud are in danger of following a similar path. They live in a world of make-believe where they act like little gods feasting on their assumed greatness while making themselves more and more impervious to any attempt to change them.

If we are consumed with pride it is easy to become arrogant and flaunt God's laws. We can convince ourselves that we know better and that we are somehow excused. Our sense of superiority can convince us of our goodness when in fact we, in concrete ways, resist the God Who would save us.

Lying

To speak the truth is a core principle of any society. Without truth all commerce and rational deliberation is not possible. Thus it is acutely alarming that from an early age the young are exposed to repeated instances of lying. Many popular TV shows display repeated lies by members of the show during presented episodes. Families engage in false narratives to avoid admitting wrongs committed. Dishonest assertions are made to gain monetary or business advantages. Books have been written referring to our "cheating culture".

An especially harmful instance of falsity is the making of charges or assertions based on little or no evidence. The smearing of a person's reputation or motives is constantly on display in the media or during public discussions. The end result is cynicism and the temptation to join in, since everyone else is doing it.

Lying is spiritually toxic. To lie is to deny truth. In small things it chips away at the fabric of our morality and leads gradually to more destructive actions. Recent dishonesty charges against celebrities in the news elicited comments by one of the perpetrators that "morality had no part in the decision to participate, only the concern of getting caught."

Without truth we lose our moorings. One lie leads to another and eventually right and wrong become "good or bad for me." Our relationship with God becomes more and more broken. We grasp at justifications for our actions, never admitting our transgressions.

Jesus came to give testimony to the Truth. We must do likewise. Otherwise we give testimony to a lie—a denial of who we are meant to be, the path we are meant to follow and the end we are created to achieve.

Minimal or Totally Lacking Prayer Life

For many, prayer is something to engage in at special times of difficulty or distress or at special family occasions—funerals, weddings, etc. For those who attend church on weekends it accompanies participation in religious services. But for most it is not an integral part of their everyday lives.

Let us examine another activity which is very prevalent in today's world—running in road races and marathons. Let us assume our participant wants to prepare for an upcoming marathon. He takes a run around the block once or twice a week and does not engage in any exercises to help him prepare to run the race. He shows up at the marathon and, as one might expect, does very poorly, probably not finishing the race. If he does finish, he very well could be included in those visiting one of the treatment tents at the end of the race, suffering pain and possibly more serious ailments.

Jesus, in one of his parables, indicated how people are quite capable of knowing how best to take care of the requirements of living in this world but are seriously lacking in looking out for their spiritual welfare. If one truly believed the words of Peter, quoted earlier—that the devil is roaming about the world looking for whom he can devour—they would put a great deal more effort into thwarting any attempts by the devil to "devour them". And one the best defenses they have available to them is prayer.

Our exemplar, Jesus, spent untold hours in prayer in preparing for His ministry and ultimately, for His passion and death on the cross. He fully realized the necessity of prayer to the Father, whereas many today do not. They have developed their own beliefs that they are somehow excused from preparing for eternity, that the merciful God will take care of them, even though they do pretty much as they please. No teaching of Jesus, no epistle from Paul or from any of the other apostles, supports such a view. In fact, it is the opposite truth which is proclaimed!

Why is prayer not more enthusiastically practiced? The answers are many. "It takes time from our busy lives". "I don't get anything out of it". "God already knows what I need".

The first purpose of prayer is worship of the God Who gave us life and has deigned to give us life with Him in eternity, if we love and obey Him. The second purpose is thanksgiving for the many gifts we have received. The third purpose is repentance, for those actions which have offended Him. And the fourth purpose is petition for what we need.

Many today do not give God the worship He deserves. They attend church only when it suits them and, I fear in many cases, their attendance is not central to their lives. I am sure that many do thank God for His many blessings that He has bestowed upon us but we must remember that we are not exempt from pain and suffering. Repentance is critical if we are to continue to grow in love and service. Such growth will allow us to see more clearly the evil of sin and whether we are indeed guilty of it. In our petition, let us ask rightly, bowing to God's wisdom and being totally accepting of His will if the answer to our requests is not forthcoming as we would like?

Those who do engage in prayer daily, who seek an ever-closer union with their God, see that the center point of their life changes from an almost total reliance on their own efforts to a greater and greater trust in God. Their stress is decreased because they are no longer attempting to bear the entire load of their trials and difficulties. They gradually see more clearly that they are pilgrims on a journey to eternity, that whatever they achieve they do so as servants fulfilling the purpose that their God has ordained for them and wanting nothing more than to serve Him.

For those who are far removed from their God and who are engaged in actions and lifestyles which are contrary to

God's law, the thought of trying to draw closer to God has little attraction since they see no way to change their current condition and think that God has abandoned them. God will never abandon them but to work toward their own salvation they must take a first step. That first step will come from the realization that God will always respond to an earnest plea for help; that His grace can remove any obstacle, clear away any doubt and show the way back to Him. The book, *Confessions of St. Augustine* gives a remarkable history of Augustine's early life of immorality and unbelief in which he relates in great detail his torturous path to a full communion with his God. Augustine lived in the early part of the 5th century and was greatly influenced by the Manichean heresy of two gods, one good and one bad. He lived a lust filled life for many years and frequently despaired that he would ever be able to live a life built on moral conduct as demanded by the Christian Faith. But through anguished prayers and repeated attempts to reform his life he found a way forward. He began to see ever more clearly God's love and his total dependence on God's grace. What is absolutely necessary is the will to begin, to pray, and to believe.

I close with the words of Jesus, "Come all ye who are heavily burdened and I will refresh you". *Mt 12:28.* Do not give up! Pray, pray unceasingly and do not lose hope. Jesus also said, "Ask and you shall receive. Seek and you shall find. Knock and it shall be opened to you". *Mt 7:7.* Jesus loves you more than you love yourself. Believe it!

Chapter Nine
Happiness

Most people want to be happy but the causes that make people happy can differ greatly. They can be as different as one man wanting great sums of money and another wanting more people to like him. The results of our childhood frequently can have strong influences in how we regard the importance of things. One could have been coddled and given everything he wanted and have grown to expect the best of everything and to have little patience in waiting for what he wanted. In contrast, one could have been very poor and bereft of even the necessities of life. That person would have lesser expectations and would be more capable of doing with less and still be relatively satisfied.

We see in the world around us extremes in desire which drive people to do many things all in the pursuit of "their happiness" but seemingly failing always to attain some sense of satisfaction in what they have achieved and what they have acquired. Not long ago I heard one TV celebrity ask another "When should I be concerned that I am striving too hard, wanting too much?" The wise response was, "when the desire to reach new heights controls and becomes the most important thing in your life."

As humans, we can allow ourselves to develop insatiable appetites, always looking for something more, yet always not achieving enough. We see financiers worth billions of dollars wanting to make more profitable ventures, sometimes even doing things illegally in the process. What could possibly cause them to blunder so outrageously? It is because they never have enough. They are driven beyond rational limits by their compulsion to make more money. We see people living much lower on the economic scale but with the same malady. The desire for more things, a higher position in life, greater prestige, can become all-consuming and over-ride more important life and family needs.

Jesus told the parable of the rich man who wanted to tear down his granaries and build new ones so that he could store his grains and live in affluence for many years. And yet that very night he was to die and leave it all behind. The old saying is, "You can't take it with you." But there is an exception. For those who believe in something more than this short sojourn on earth there is something that they can take with them—love. But they don't take it all with them. They leave behind the love they gave others, the seeds of love they planted in helping others to live better lives, more fulfilling lives—lives, in turn, which will produce an out flowing of love for years to come.

From a Christian perspective, this world is a "vale of tears." Many in our country have not seen this vale of tears, at least not initially when they grew up. They experienced no hardships and life was good. And that was a great blessing! But sometimes I fear we come to believe that we are special and that God has ordained that that good times should always continue and that we should never encounter that "vale of tears." When something bad happens how often do we hear, "How can God allow that to happen? A loving God should have prevented that from occurring!" To say something like that is to indicate a serious lack in understanding of the world we live in. Bad things do happen due to natural evils and due to other human beings, intent on furthering their own desires. We cannot change this, though we can work to ameliorate the effects. We can also not let the world keep us from our most important task, becoming the best we can be as full and loving human beings.

To do this we must have faith, a faith that there is meaning in life, that we are on a journey to a better life. This is the essence of Christianity. We have a stake in the outcome and we have a responsibility to account for our actions. We cannot just assume that somehow God will take care of us. We must also realize that our actions will have consequences in this life. Though it is true that many things will occur that are beyond our control, many others will be the direct result of what we do or do not do. If we do foolish things we can expect the result of foolish things! If we put ourselves in harm's way we may experience the harm we could have avoided. Actions have consequences! It bears repeating over and over.

How do we summarize what I am trying to say? Love your neighbor as yourself. Do not hurt your neighbor *and* do not hurt yourself. To this I should add, don't beat up on yourself as part of a guilt trip—"I'm no good, I don't deserve to be forgiven", etc. This is really a cop-out. If a person is really no good then they can feel justified in just giving up. They can make themselves believe that even God will not forgive them.

But this is a big lie. God wants more than you can know for you to become whole again. But you must take a first step. You must believe that there is hope. You must believe that you will be given the strength to not take the next drink, to not try that drug that everyone tells you will give you some super high. You must come to believe that you can grow in love of others, and very importantly, of yourself.

Do you want to be happy? Then act like you want to be happy! Understand the ways you want to be happy and choose those ways that will really make you happy, rather than those ways which will actually make you unhappy.

PART THREE

Introduction

At a recent homily at Mass I heard the celebrant ask how many in the congregation wanted to go to heaven. Virtually everyone raised their hands. Then he asked, "How many of you want to go today?" He got no takers.

Change is always difficult, but a transition from life to death is change par excel lance! We know this life. We conjecture about the future life because we do not know. The question is always about faith. The greater our faith the less apprehension we have. St. Monica, the mother of St. Augustine, told him one day after she witnessed his conversion (something she had prayed for over 30 years) that she had no more interest in living. She believed that her work was done and that she was ready to meet her God. Her faith had removed any doubts and she anticipated the eternal joy of being with God forever.

We all have a choice. We can wait for that inevitable day when we will make that transition to eternity and accept it as it comes with little thought ahead of time. Or we can make our preparation in the best way we can. Like most transitions we experience in life, they will precede better if we prepare better. So let us begin.

Chapter One
The Joy of Hope

We live in a world where pleasure is paramount. Onerous tasks and self-denial are frowned upon and are to be engaged in only when absolutely necessary. Living a disciplined life and making an effort to improve ourselves spiritually are tasks deemed by many to be very difficult and not intrinsically rewarding.

The young are especially vulnerable to seek pleasurable things because they often do not have the experience to value the better way. When I was a child, I especially loved to eat the frosting on the cake much more than the cake itself. I would see my father scrape off some of the frosting before he ate his cake and I never could understand why he did that. Today I do just what my father did!

Maybe you're not yet ready to avoid eating much of your frosting but I suspect that you have many other things you would prefer to eat more than frosting. On an intellectual level we can expect there to be similar differences between what activities we enjoy as we get older compared to those activities we were passionate about when we were young. The same can be true of our values. If we have taken the time to evaluate those things we have found really important in our lives, we may have seen that the goals and accomplishments we had on our "to do list" when we were younger have changed.

The focus of this chapter is "joy" as opposed to "pleasure". The child experiences sensual pleasure as he eats his frosting. His mother has the emotion of joy when she sees how happy he is to receive presents and eat birthday cake on another anniversary. The older we are the less we are moved by pleasure, which we know is fleeting and even in some ways harmful. Joy, on the other hand, is much deeper, more totally absorbing. It does not ebb and flow like the tide, but it builds as we more fully realize and comprehend the source of that joy,

So how is one to effectively increase in joy—"that bright spark of Divinity"—immortalized in the chorus of Beethoven's Ninth Symphony? It is through grace, the free gift of God, without which we cannot succeed. Grace is like water flowing over a parched landscape providing the nourishing revitalization of a dormant earth. But if the crust of the soil is so hard the water flows past and does no good. What is required is porosity which allows the water to penetrate and begin the needed renewal.

The human soul is thirsting for the Divine spark which will revitalize a dormant existence. But there must be some accommodation by the soul to receive and embrace the Divine gift. If there is hardness of heart, if there is the infestation of evil then there may well be no change. But if a sliver of light is allowed in, if there is a crack in the hardness then there can be a response.

Our task then is to respond to the graces we receive so that we can grow in faith and love. Until we arrive at our eternal home we will not fully comprehend what awaits us but we can grow in hope. But the hope must be grounded in faith and a greater and greater awareness of the Truth. Thus, on a spiritual basis we start with faith, which in turn builds love and engenders hope. If that faith is nourished and valued it will grow and become more integral with who we are. We will see ever more clearly where we are going and why we are going—toward the source of all, God.

St. Paul writes that, "for Christ's sake I have accepted the loss of all things and I consider them as so much rubbish that I may gain Him". *Phil 3:8.* It is this realization that fosters greater and greater hope. Those who work to build their faith and grow in love will in turn grow in hope, and that greater hope will fill them with the joy and anticipation of possessing God forever.

Chapter Two
On the Threshold of Eternity

The most important choice anyone will ever make is what course they choose at the moment of death. The reality is that much of that choice will have frequently been made long before the moment of death. Let me explain.

There are any number of ways that people prepare for death, some definitive and many of a default nature. Take for example a daredevil who believes in living life on the edge, engaging in dangerous activities that could lead to death at any time. An accidental slip, a miscalculation, an unforeseen occurrence and that person's life is over. He probably has spent little time, if any, thinking about what happens after death. If one were to have asked him beforehand about his possible death he likely would have brushed off further discussion with a shrug or with some bravado or flippant statement like, "C'est la vie."

Some who are declared atheists perhaps have avoided any discussion at all, considering such discussion a tunnel leading nowhere. Or perhaps they have heard of novel ideas like freezing their body, or as I heard recently, just their brain, so that science could in some distant future bring them or part of them back to life.

More commonly, people do make some preparations, especially if they have been ill for some time. Religious belief has an important part in any preparation, leading some to a peaceful and hopeful expectation of the afterworld. But unfortunately, that religious experience not infrequently has led others to abandon any belief they may have had and pass from life enmeshed in a state of angry denial of God or anything connected with life after death.

Many other possibilities could be mentioned but the important point to be made is to emphasize the need to arrive at a personal and satisfactory answer to the following question, "Do I believe in a life after death and in accordance with that belief have I taken steps to leave this earthly life in the best way I can to conform to the requirements of that belief?"

In arriving at an answer to the above question we must be scrupulously honest with ourselves. It is tempting to hear what we want to hear when presented with the realities of life and death. We can say yes to some things but refuse to fully agree with others. We can make excuses or indulge in altering our beliefs so as to make the requirements less arduous. And we might say, "Doesn't God love me and won't He understand why I just can't act that way?"

I would like at this point to repeat just a few thoughts that I presented earlier. You can accept or reject them but I hope you will at least consider them and pray about them. God is the source of all love and all goodness. Before we were created there was the eternal God, and after creation is past and we come to the end of time (a created reality) there will be God with all of the created human beings living with him forever. But to be with God we will need to be filled with the love of God and to have endured the trial of this life, to have chosen to be with God forever and have renounced evil. Those who have chosen evil will be separated from God and will be in a place without love.

Since we really don't have any idea as to what to expect in the afterlife, I suggest that we quietly think about the words of St. Paul in his Epistle to the Corinthians, "Eye has not seen, ear has not heard, nor has it entered into the heart of man the things which God has prepared for those who love Him." *1 Cor 2:9.* That appears to be something worth working toward!

When we reach eternal life, we will know the state we are in and we will receive the recompense for what we have done. There will be no excuses. There will be no second chance. If we have taken shortcuts, if we have been insincere, we will know and God will know.

What state will we want to be in when we reach the moment of death? Let us hope that we have incessantly searched for wisdom and understanding; that we have become filled with love of God and our neighbor; that as we stand at the edge of eternity, would that we would yearn to hear the eternal words, "Come ye blessed of my Father and inherit the kingdom prepared for you from the foundation of the world." *Mt 25:34.*

Let us make the right choice. Let us choose eternal bliss and thank God for all eternity that we have done so!

BIBLIOGRAPHY

The New American Bible, St. Joseph Edition (The Catholic Book Publishing Co., New York, 1986).

Amorth, Gabriel. *An Exorcist Tells His Story* (Ignatius Press, San Francisco, 1999).

—. *An Exorcist, More Stories* (Ignatius Press, San Francisco, 2002).

Bennett, Rod. *The Four Witnesses* (Ignatius Press, San Francisco, 2002).

Benedict XVI. Encyclical Letter, *Saved by Hope, 2007.*

Brother Benignus. *Nature, Knowledge and God* (The Bruce Publishing Co., Milwaukee, 1947).

Carroll, Warren. *The Founding of Christendom* (Christendom Press, Front Royal, Va., 1983).

—. *The Building of Christendom* (Christendom Press, Front Royal, Va., 1985).

—. *The Glory of Christendom* (Christendom Press, Front Royal, Va., 1993).

—. *The Cleavage of Christendom (Christendom Press, Front Royal, Va., 2000).*

Crowley, Roger. *Empires of the Sea (Random House, Inc., New York, 2008).*

Flew, Anthony. *There is a God* (Harper Collins, New York, 2007).

Howell, Kenneth. *Clement of Rome: the Didache* (CHResources, Zanesville, OH, 2012).

Keller, Verner. *The Bible as History* (A Bantam Book, William Morrow and Co. 1974).

Lewis, Bernard. *The Middle East* (A Touchstone Book, Simon and Schuster, New York, 1995).

Limbaugh, David. *The Emmaus Code* (Regnery Publishing, Washington, DC, 2015).

McKenzie, S.J., John. *The Two-edged Sword* (Image Books, Doubleday and Co., Garden City, N.Y., 1955).

Meldau, Fred. *The Prophets Still Speak, Messiah in Both Testaments* (Bellmawr, NJ, 1988).

Saint Augustine. *Confessions of St. Augustine* (Sheed and Ward, 1943).

Schroeder, Gerald. *The Science of God* (Free Press, New York, 1997)

www.ingramcontent.com/pod-product-compliance
Lightning Source LLC
Chambersburg PA
CBHW060535130626
46553CB00002B/765